Anna Haifisch
Mouse in Residence

Spector Books

Translated by James Turek

"Don't count the mice before they've moved
into your house."

German proverb

"The relevance of an artistic work created in seclusion will have to succumb to the alternative visions of the polycultural."

Cole Mountain Association of
Painting and Pewter Wares

"Our residency program can not keep up with
the infrastructure of the post-global urban world.
We are fully aware of that. And yet, for some
wishing to find freedom, security, and prosperity,
Fahrenbuhl is the last beacon of hope."

Fahrenbuhl Endowment for the Arts

"A stay in Fahrenbuhl does not make sense
for everyone."

Minister of State for Cultural
and Economic Affairs

"In Fahrenbuhl I want to transform into a
 different mouse."

                              Mouse in Residence

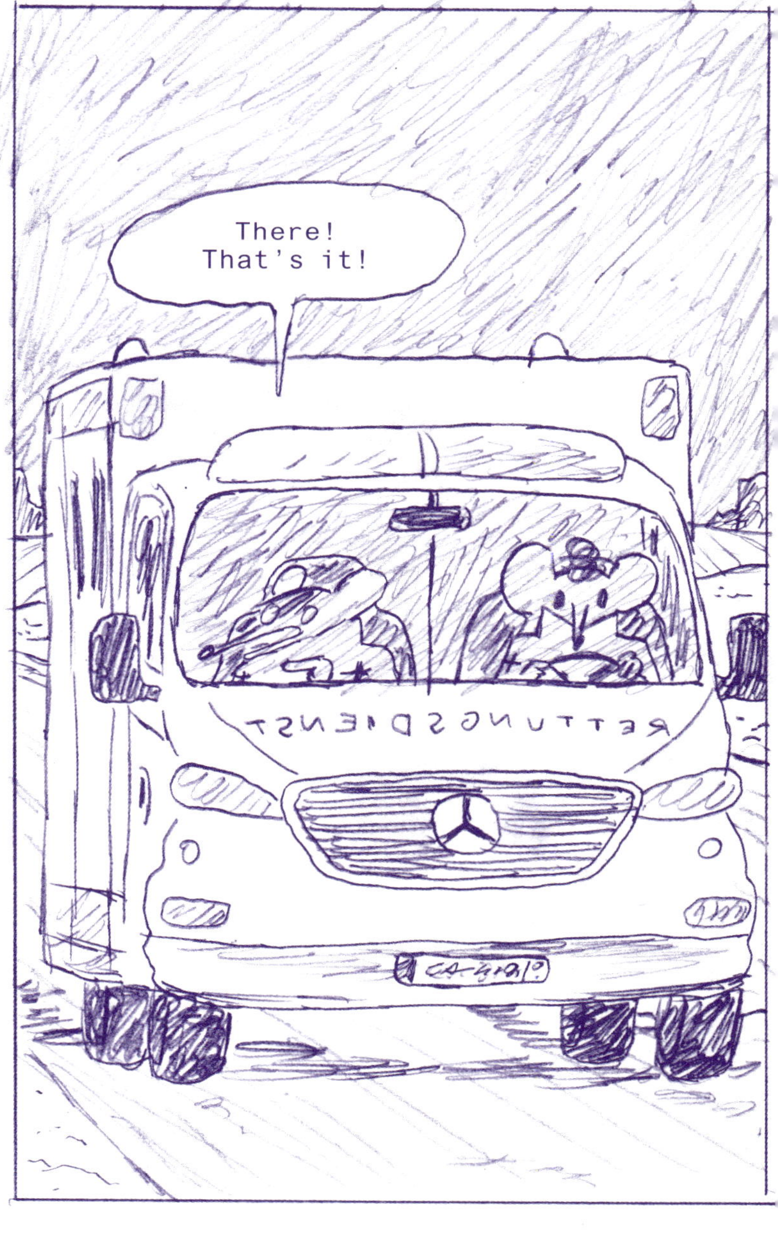

There!
That's it!
RETTUNGSDIENST

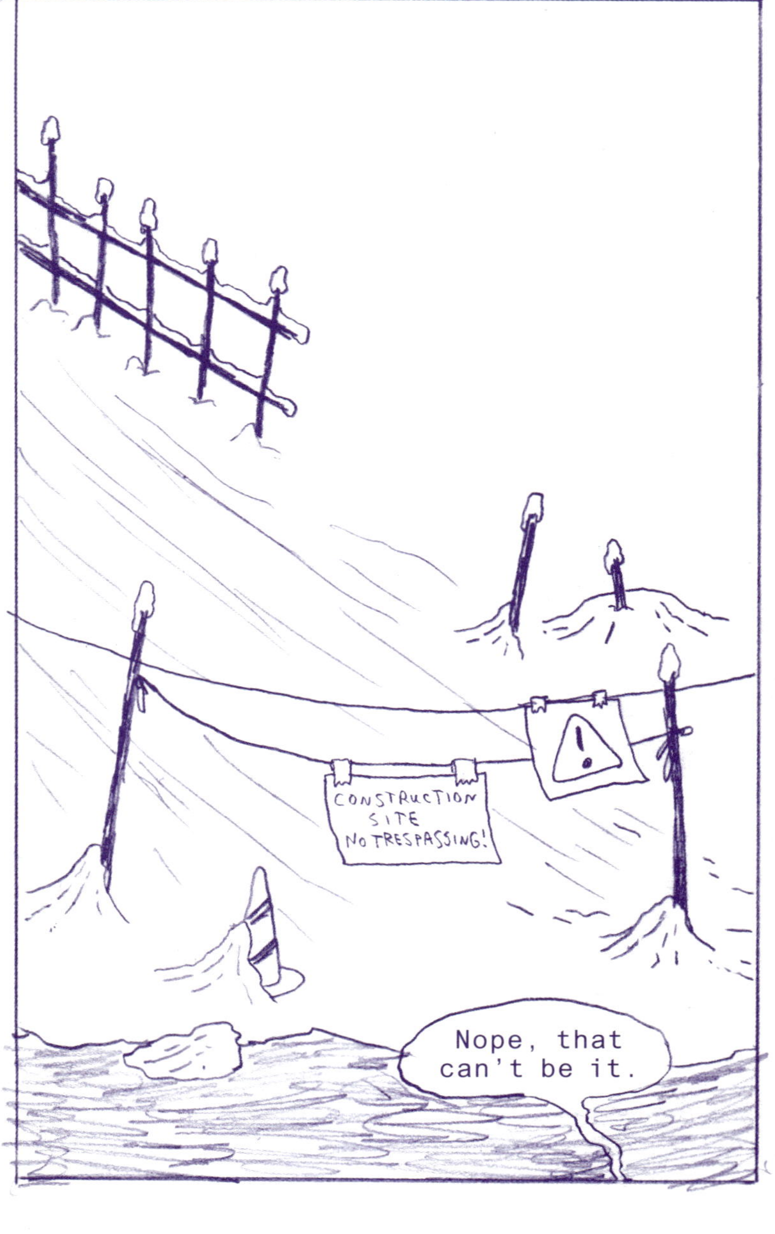

CONSTRUCTION
SITE
NO TRESPASSING!

Nope, that
can't be it.

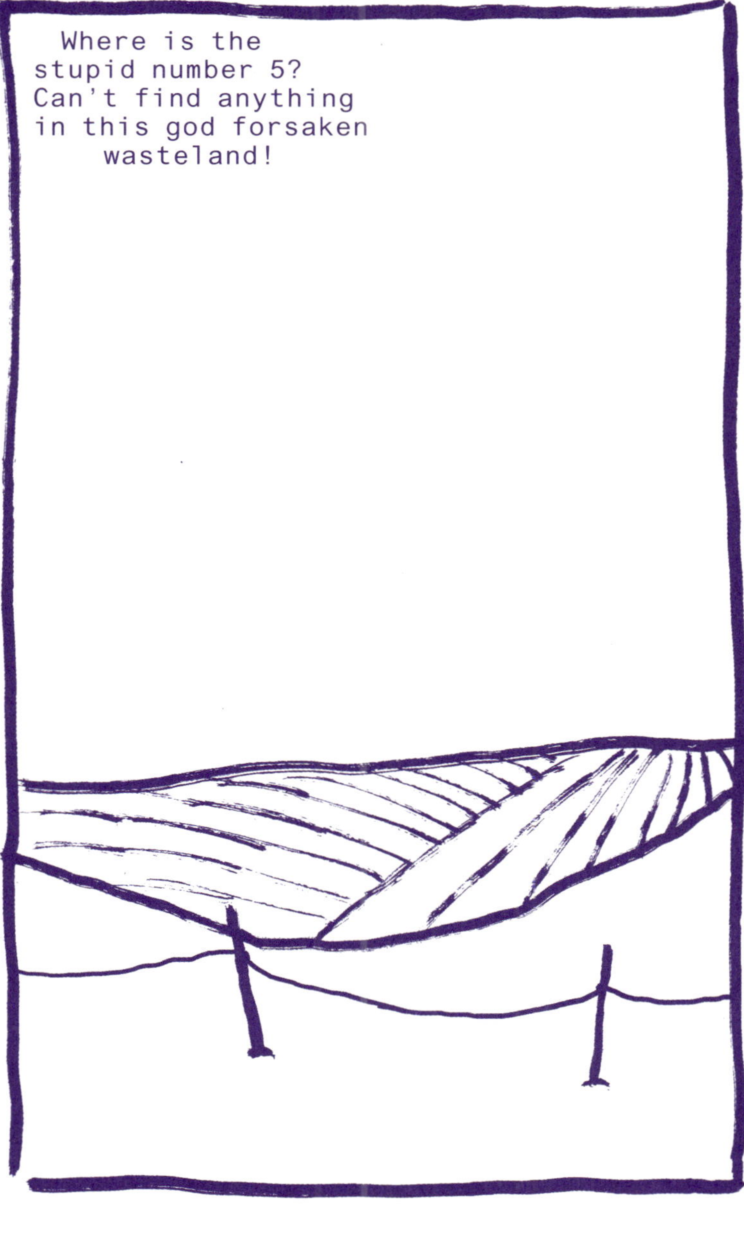
Where is the
stupid number 5?
Can't find anything
in this god forsaken
wasteland!

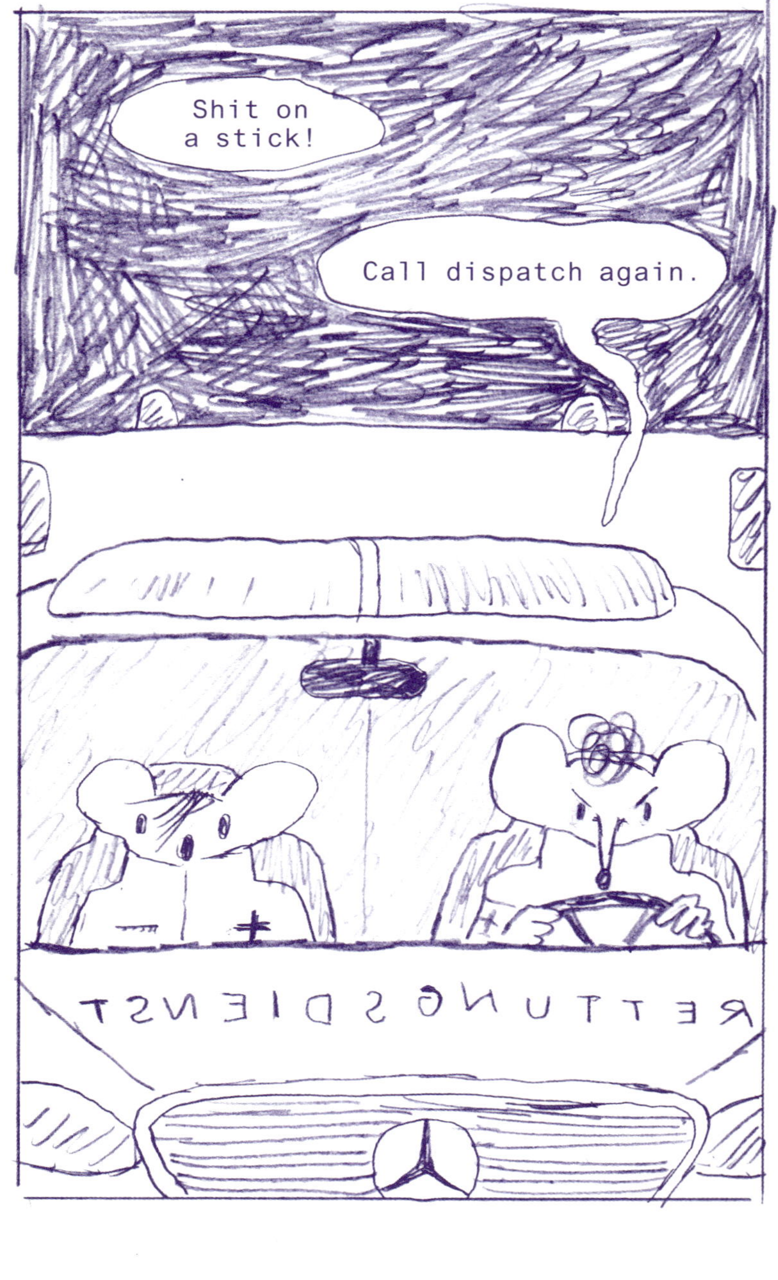

Shit on
a stick!
Call dispatch again.
RETTUNGSDIENST

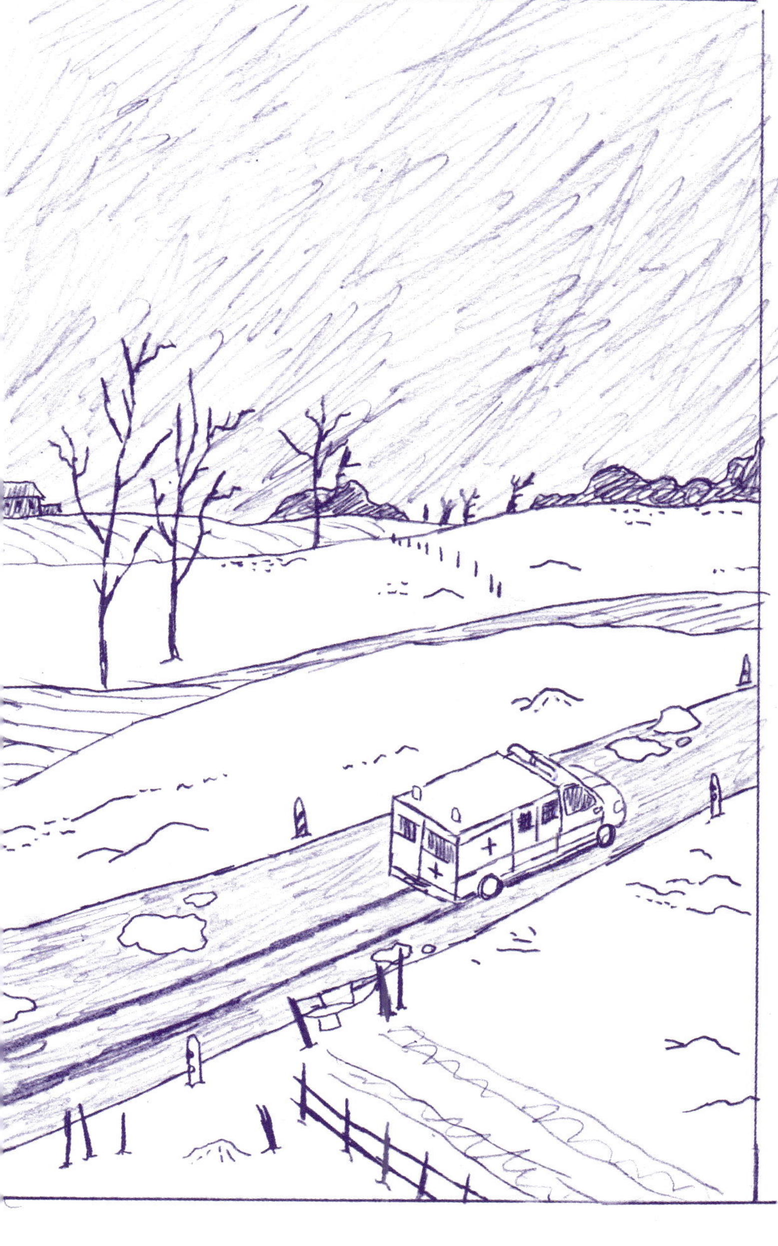

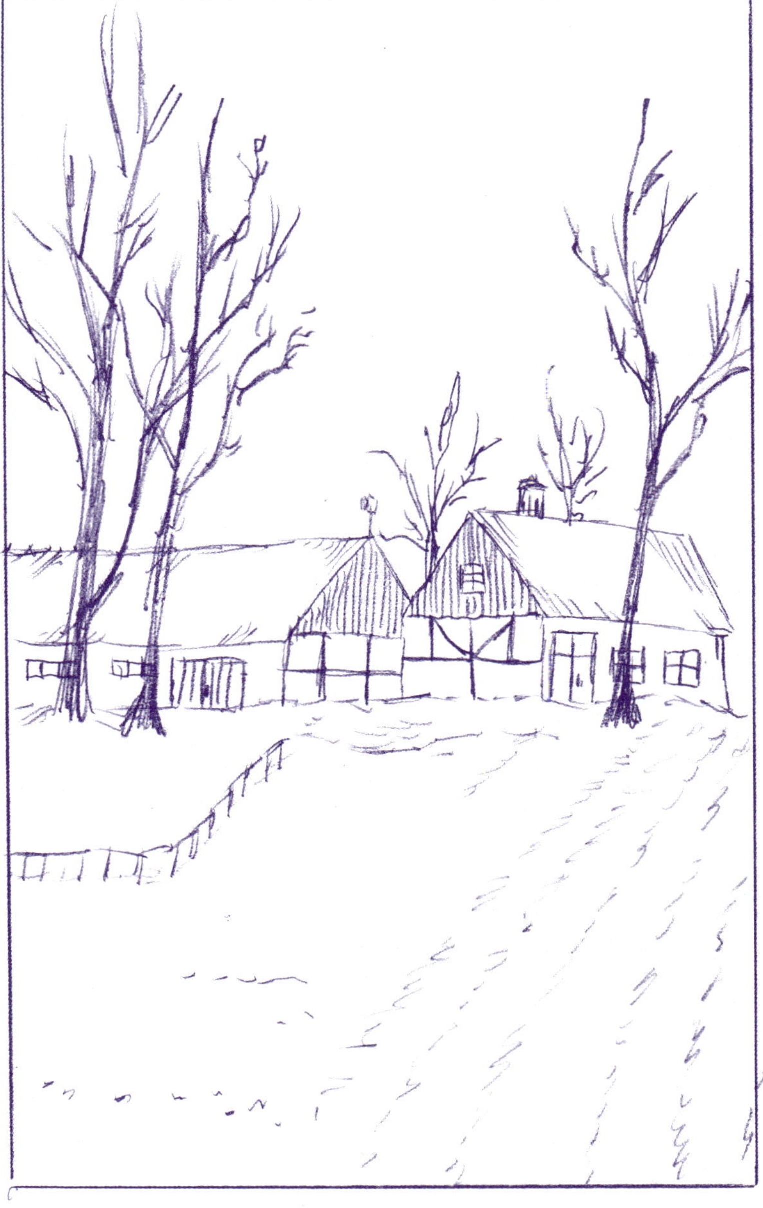

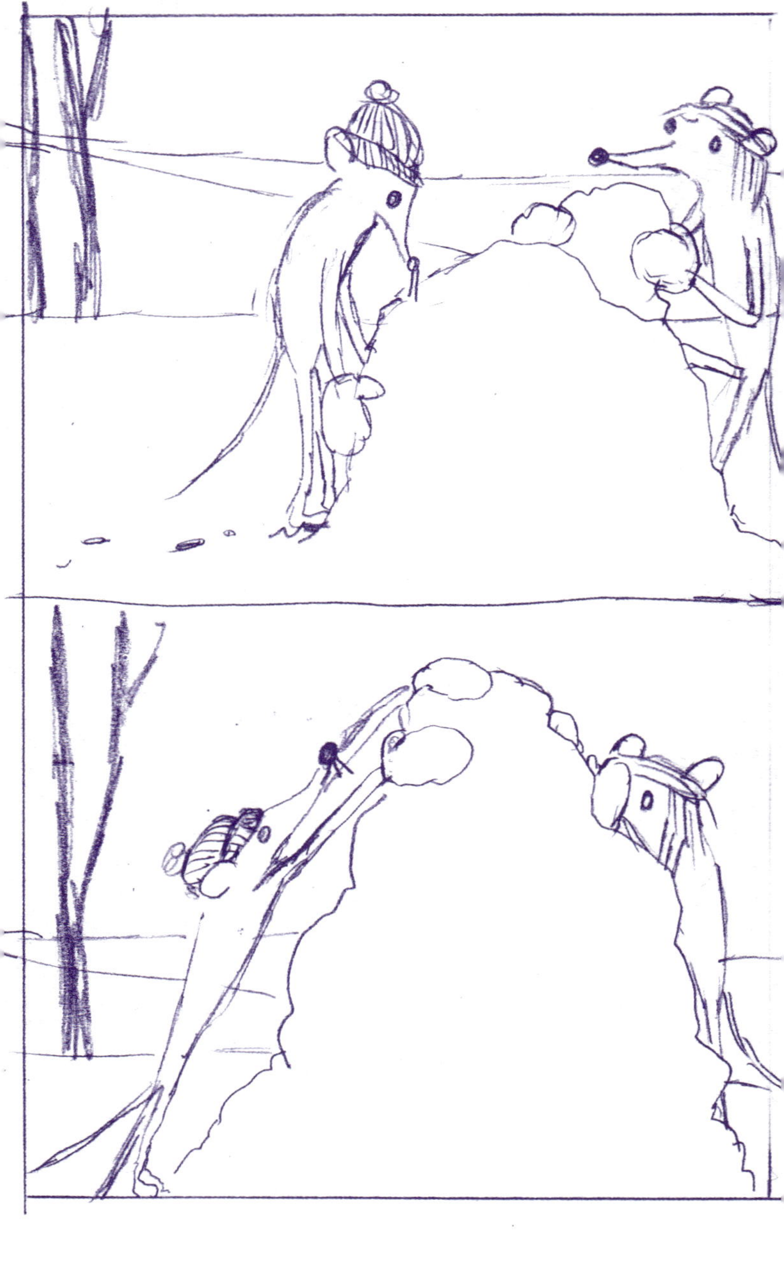

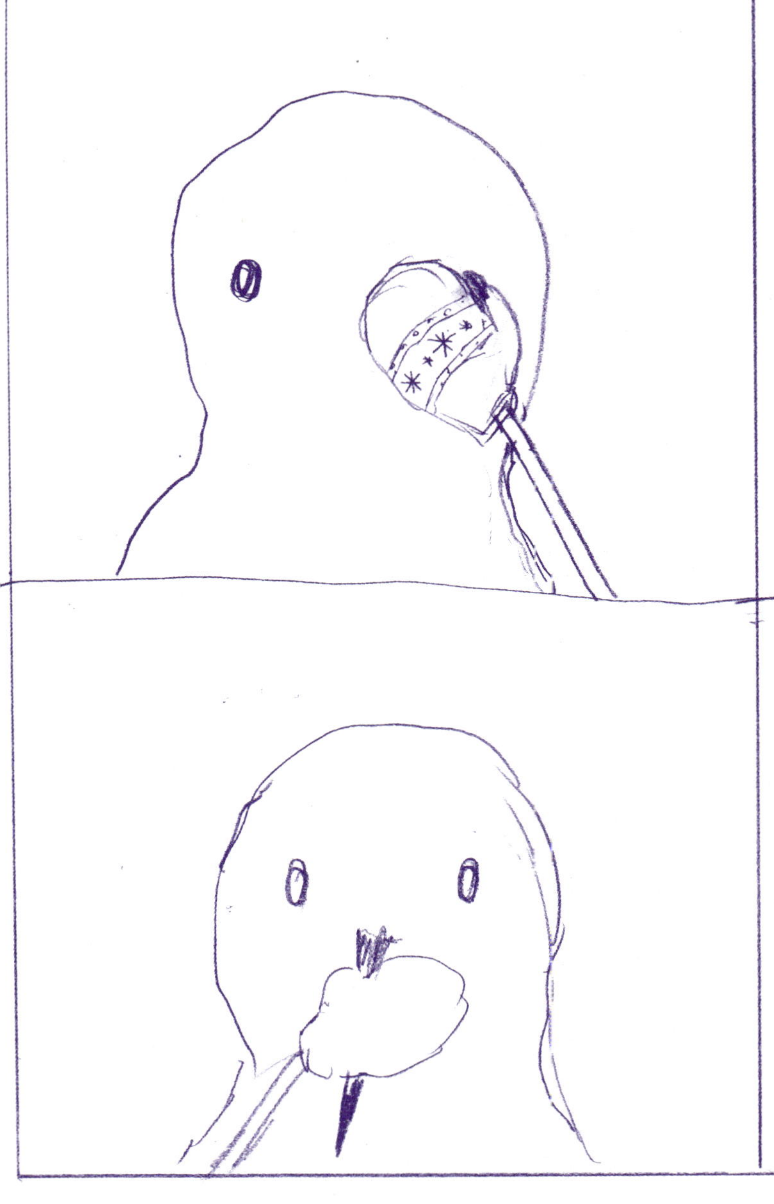

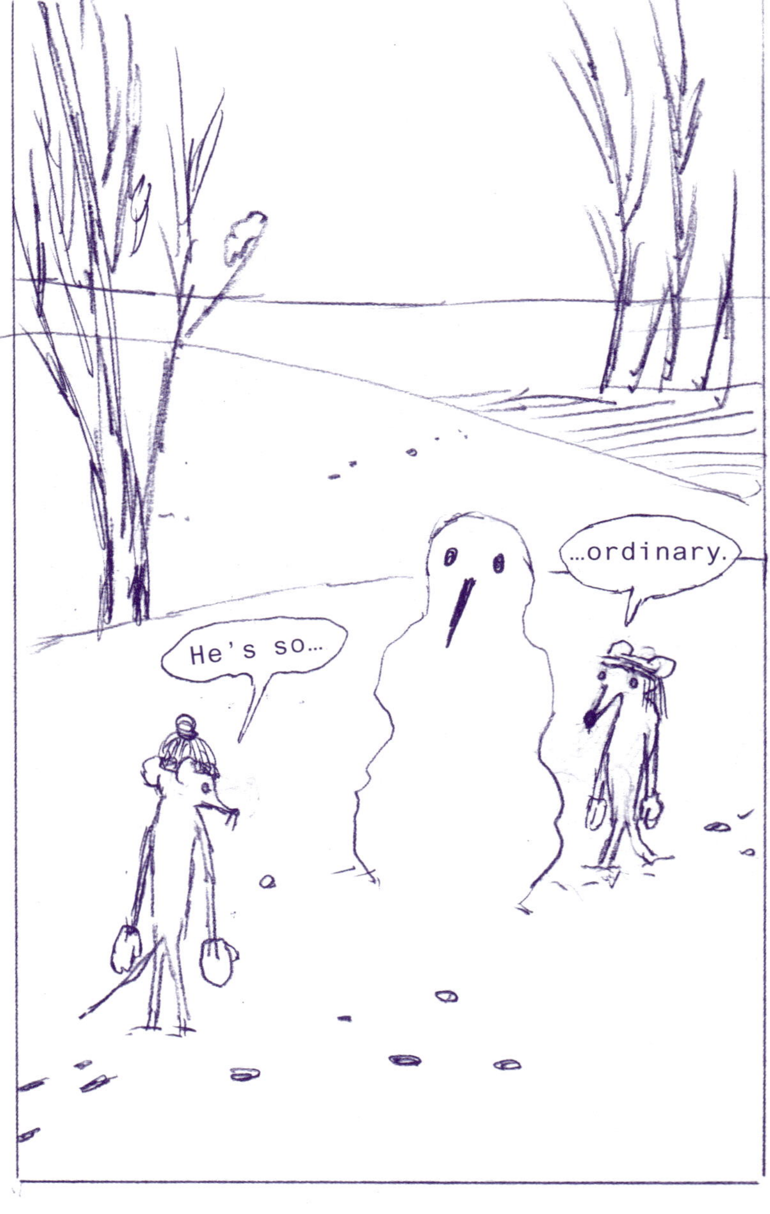
...ordinary.
He's so...

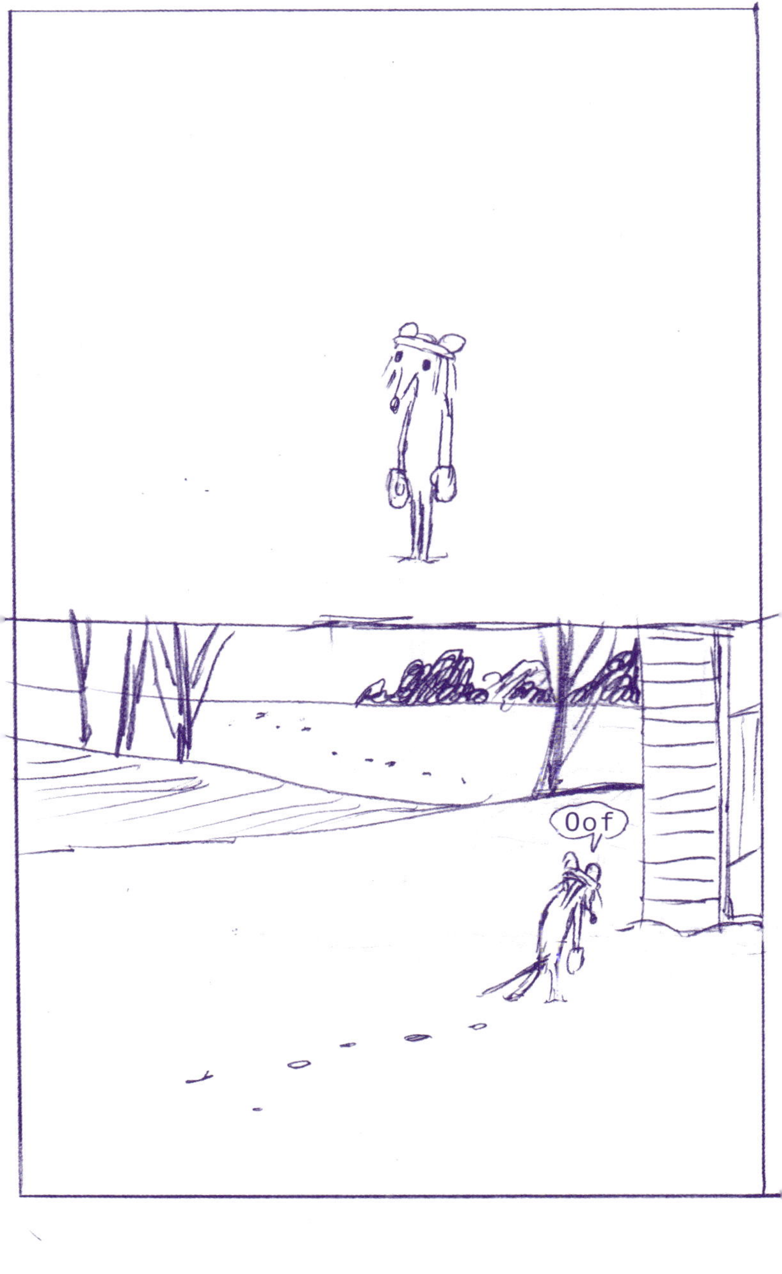

Oof

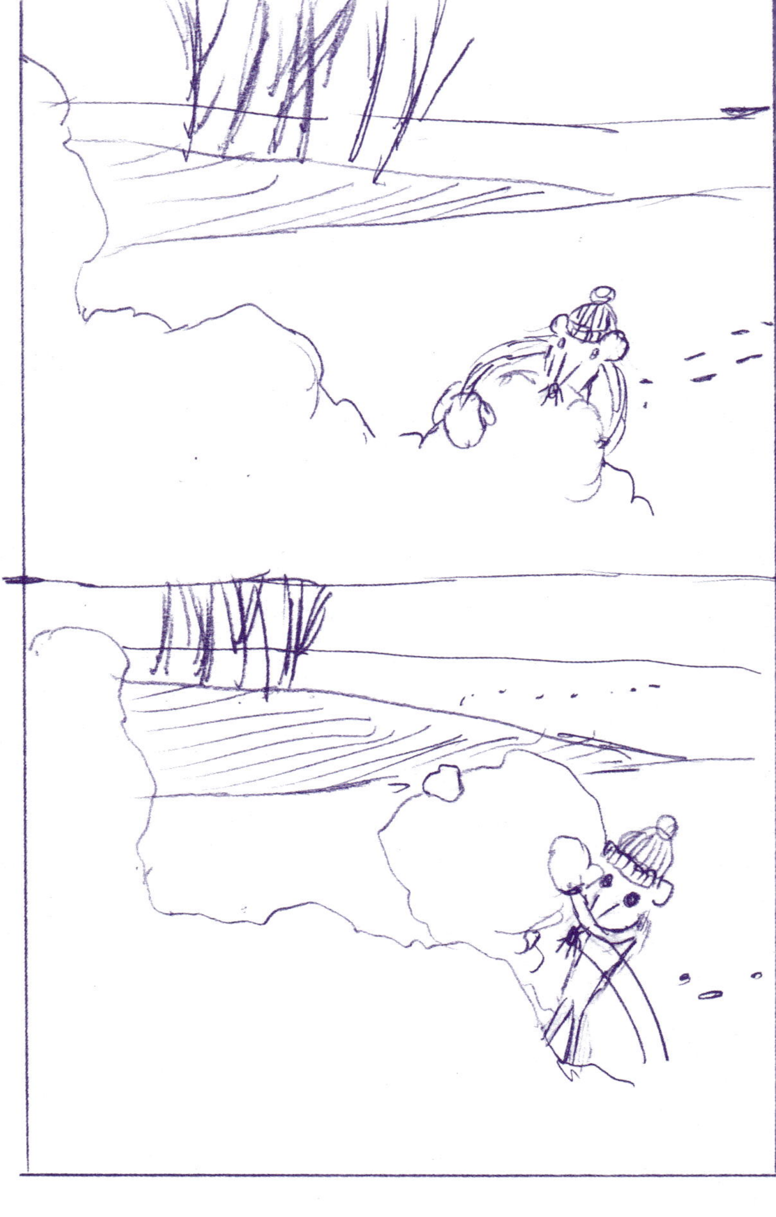

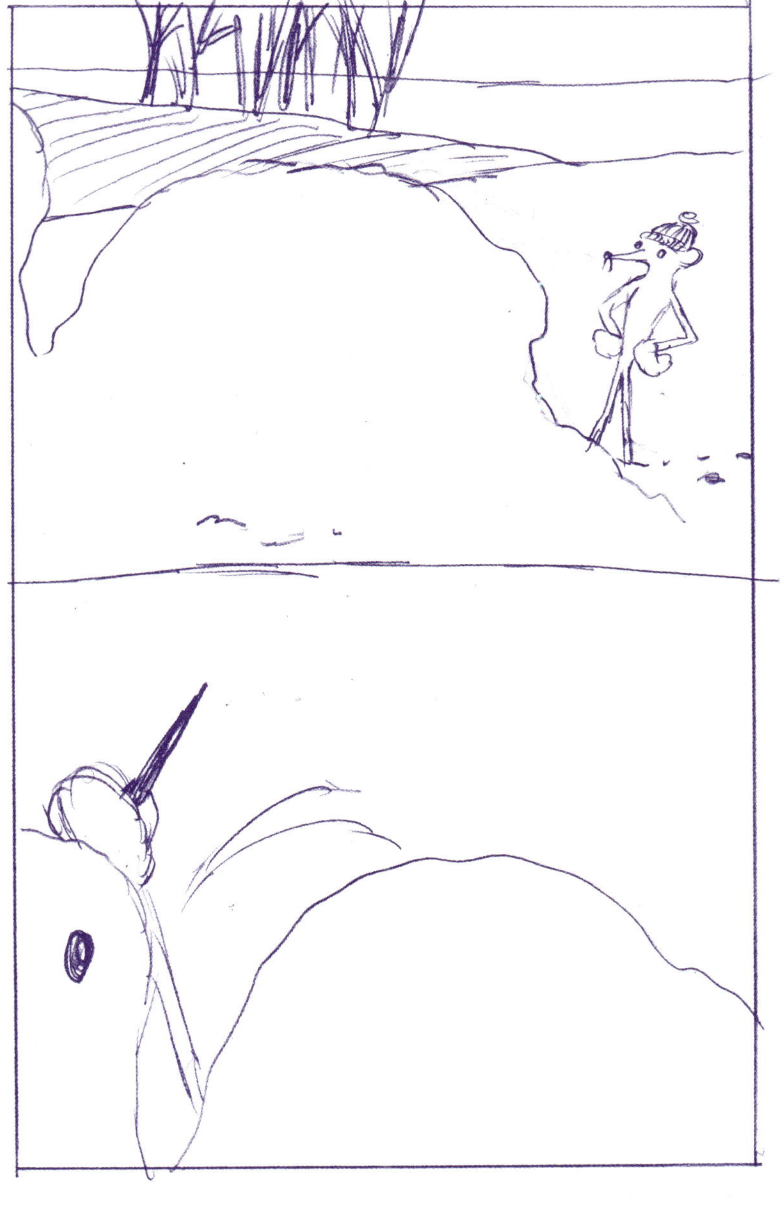

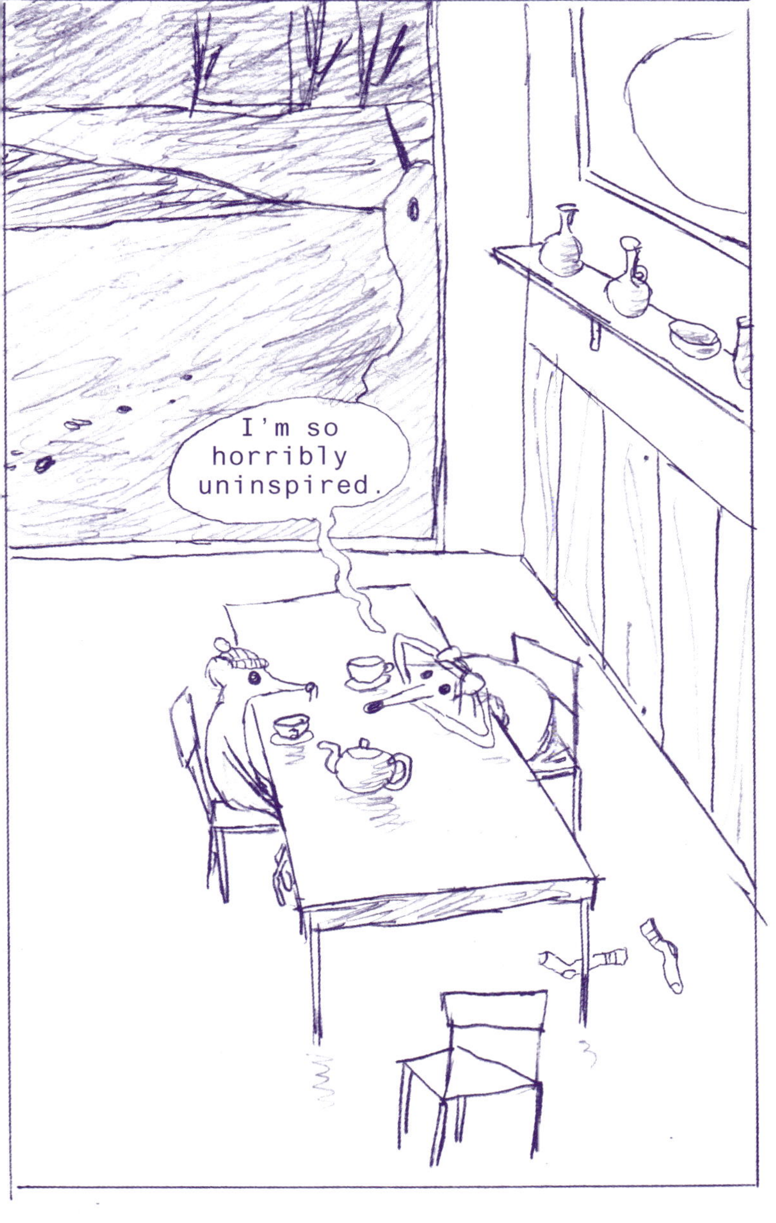

I'm so horribly uninspired.

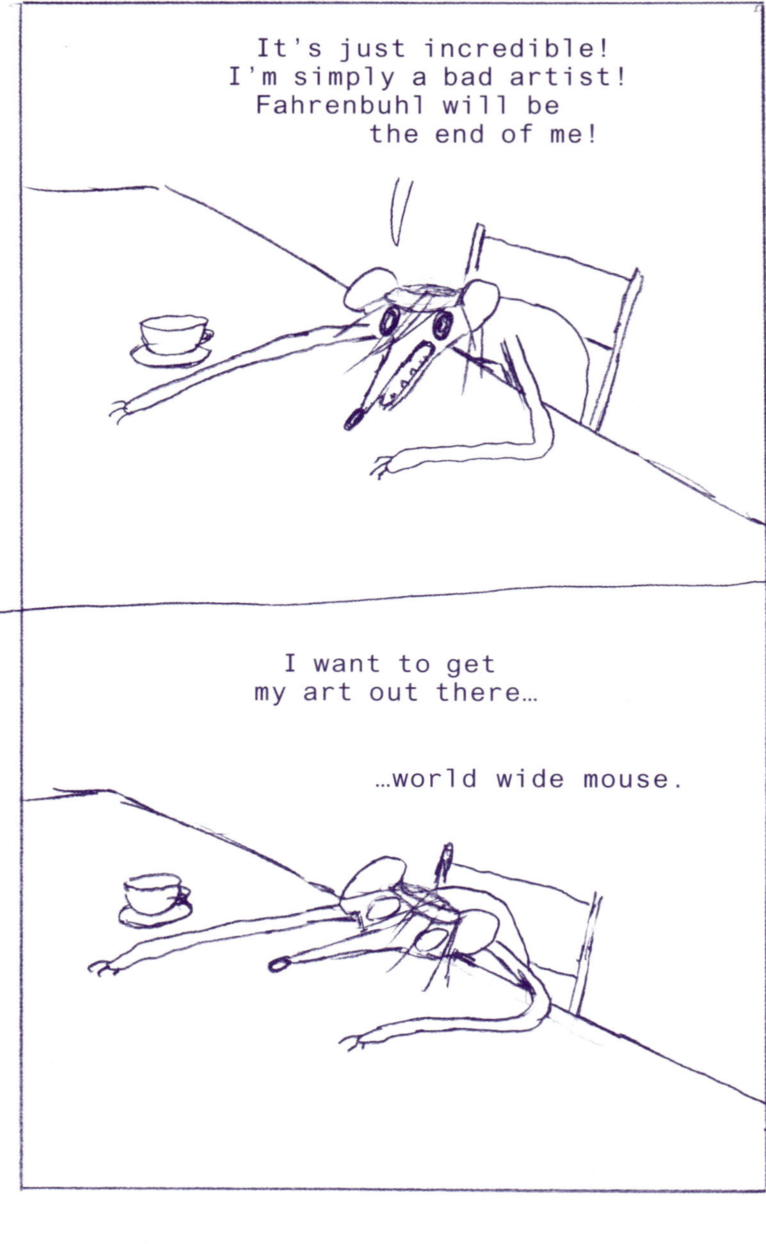
It's just incredible!
I'm simply a bad artist!
Fahrenbuhl will be
the end of me!
I want to get
my art out there...
...world wide mouse.

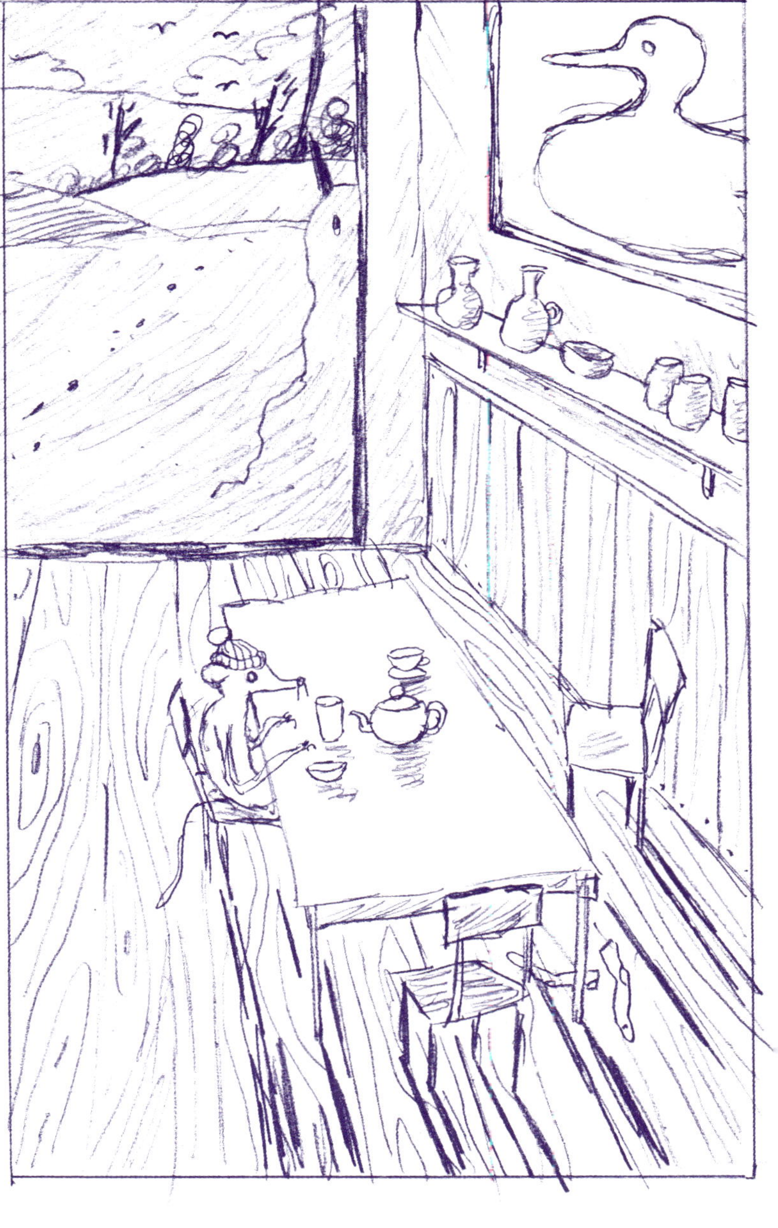

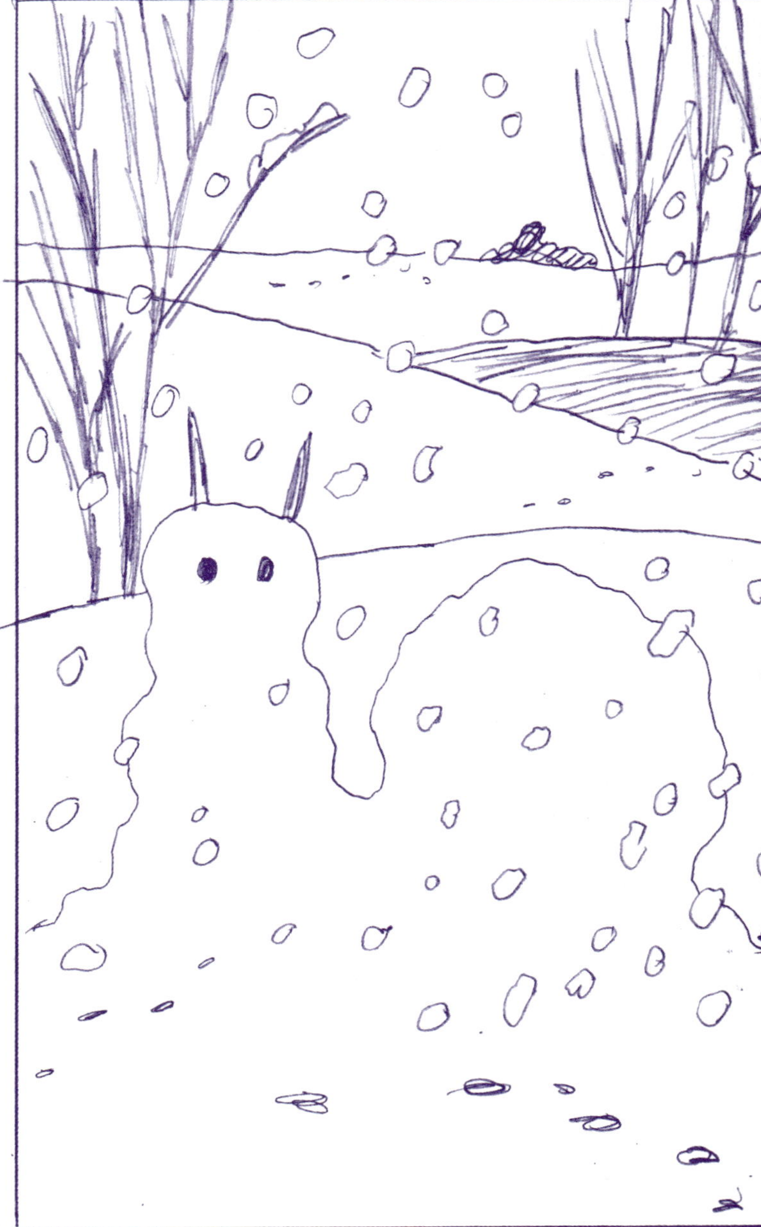

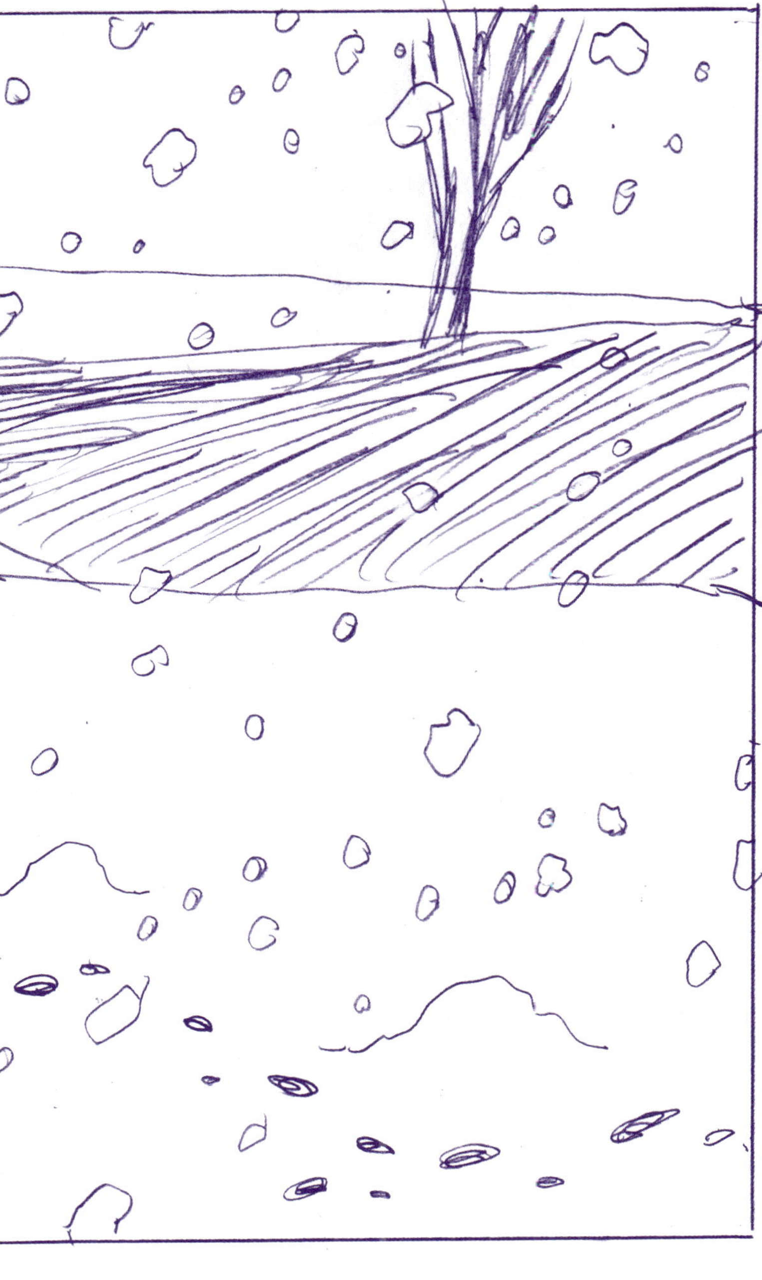

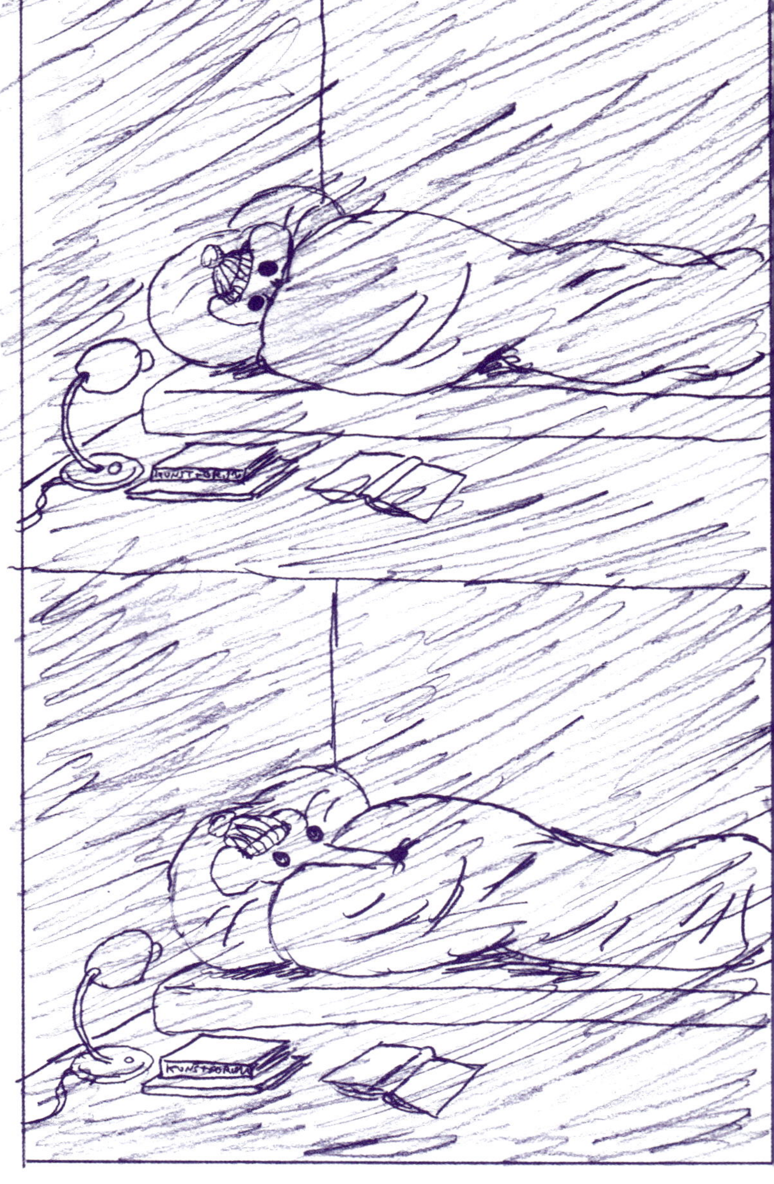
KUNSTFORUM
KUNSTFORUM

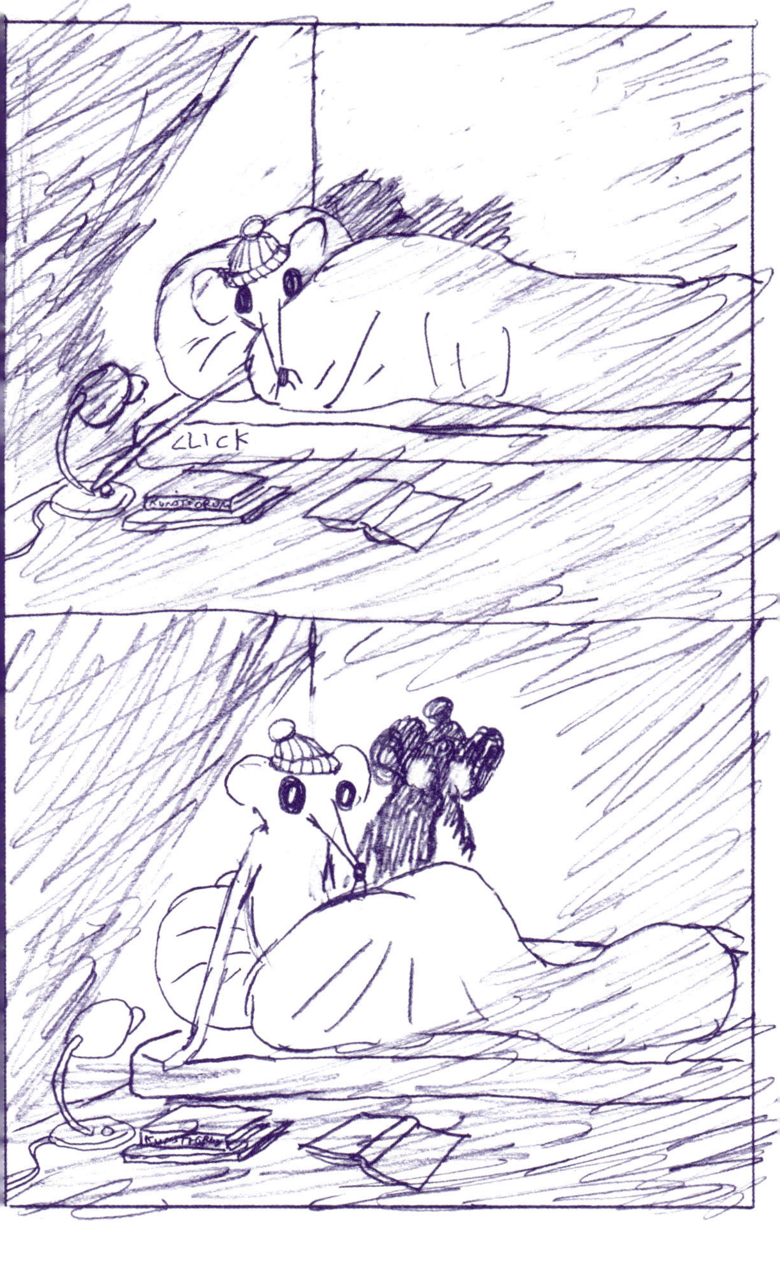

CLICK

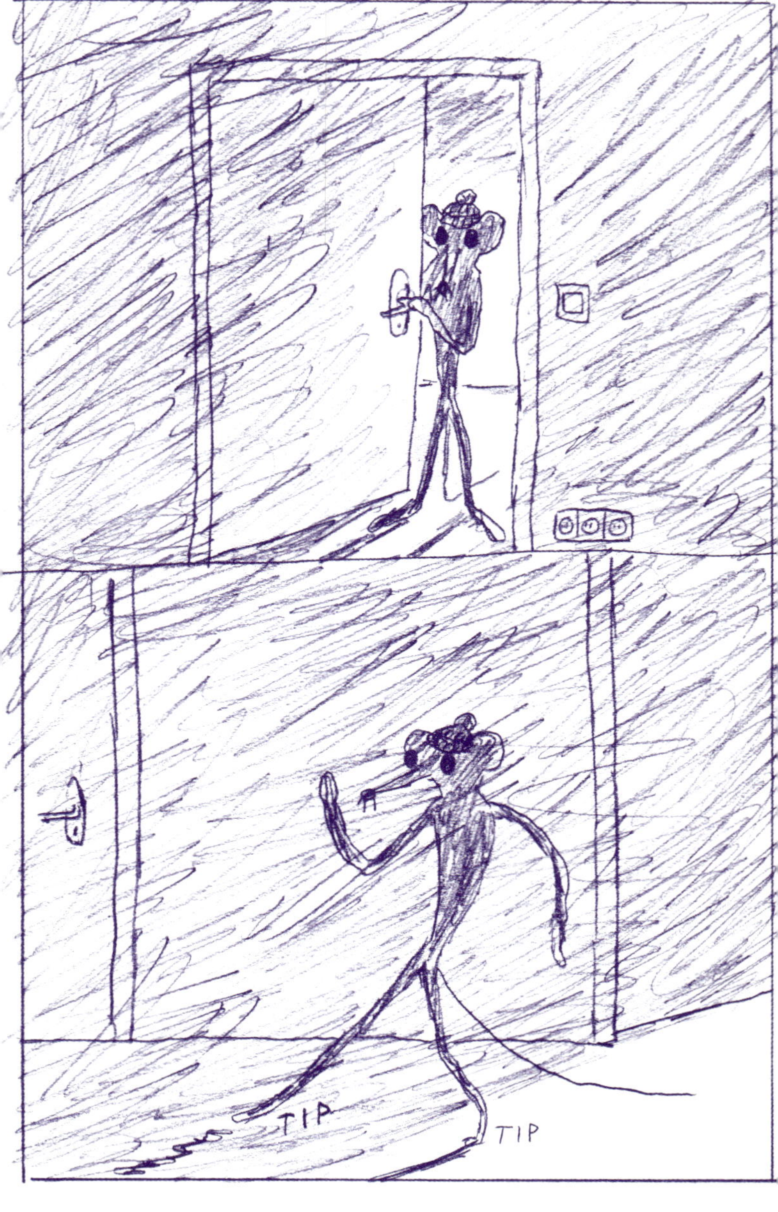
TIP
TIP

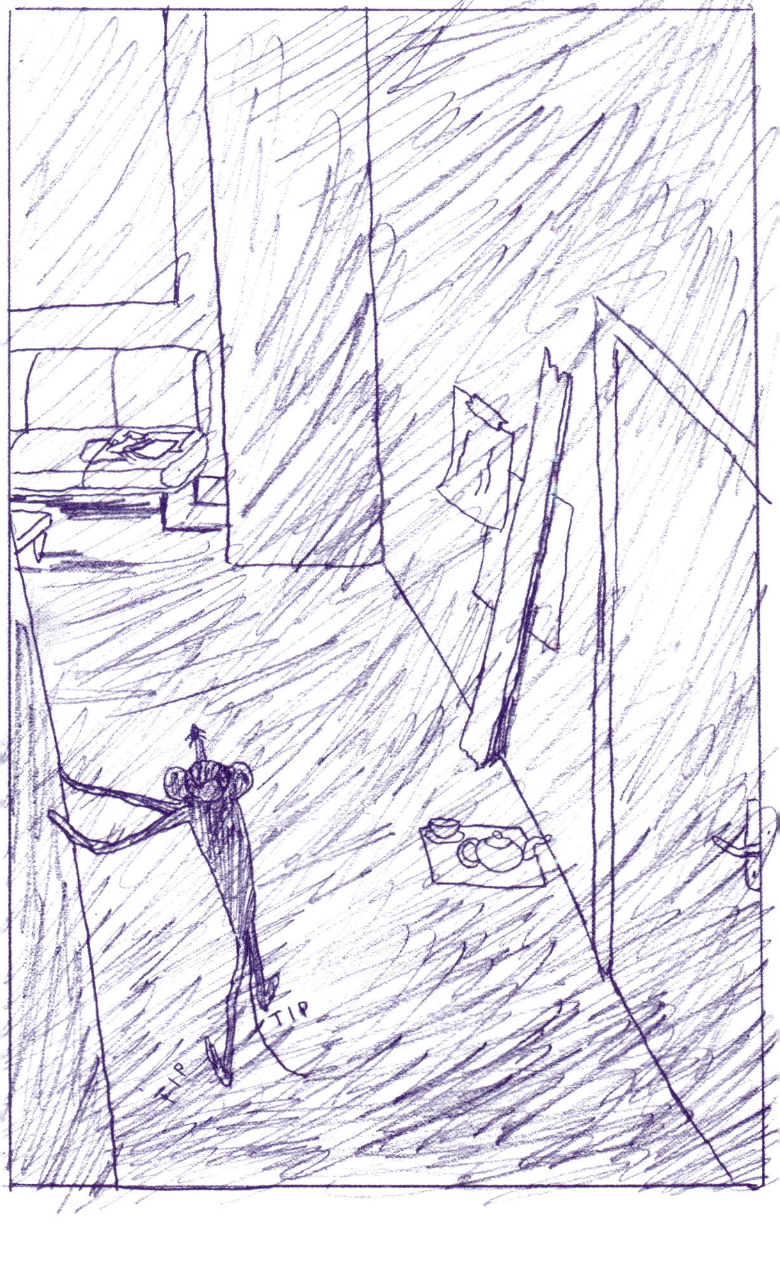

TIP
TIP

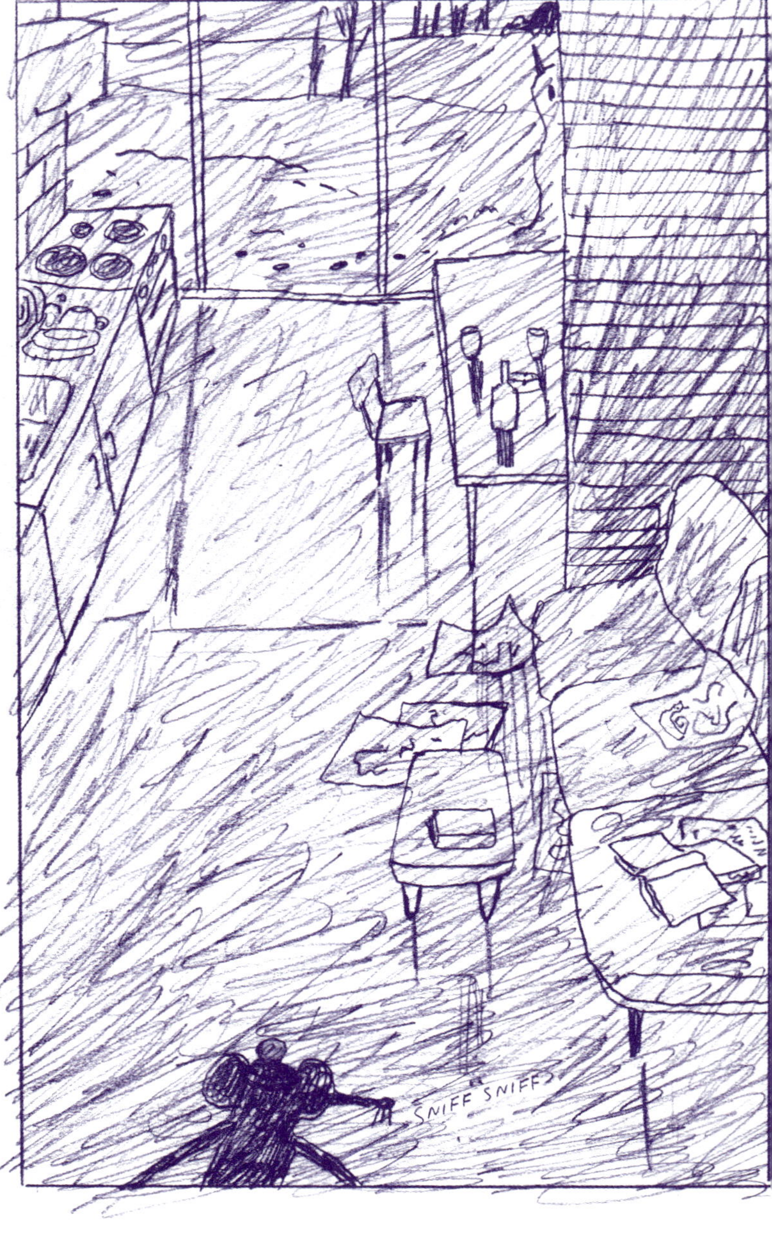
SNIFF
SNIFF SNIFF

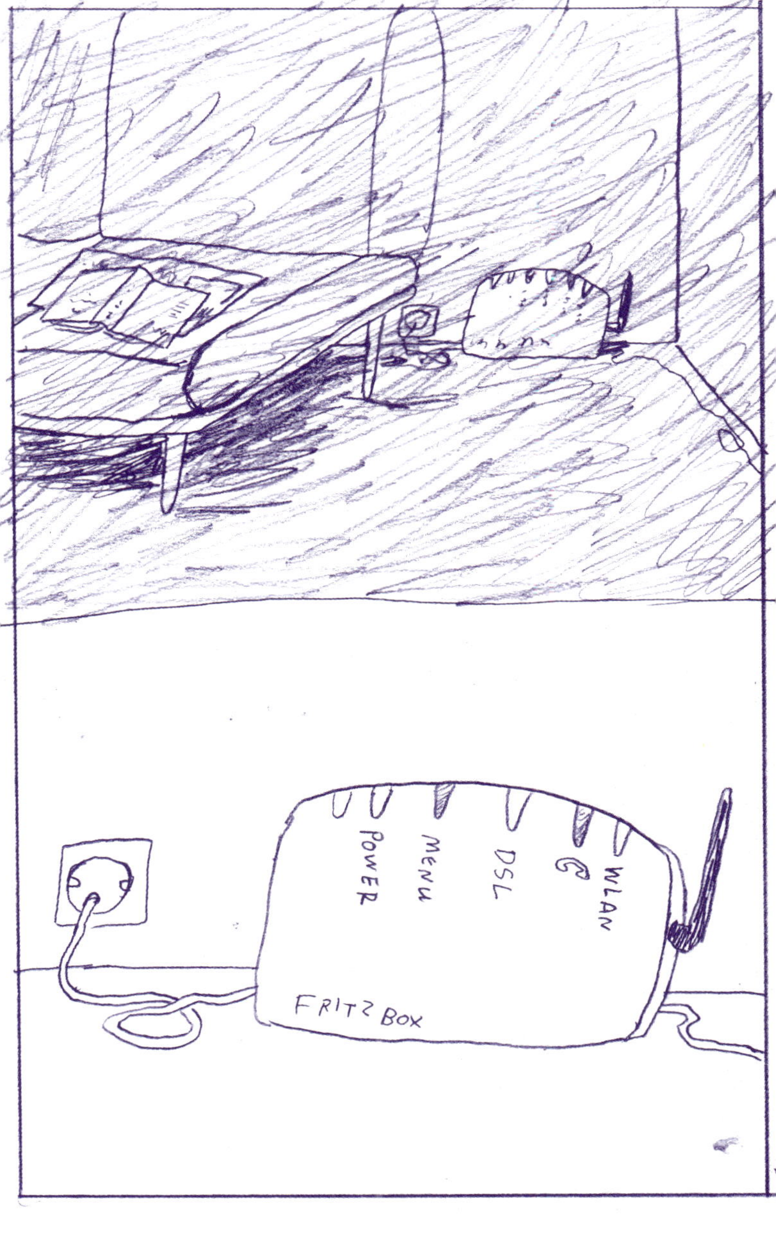

WLAN
DSL
Menu
Power
FRITZ Box

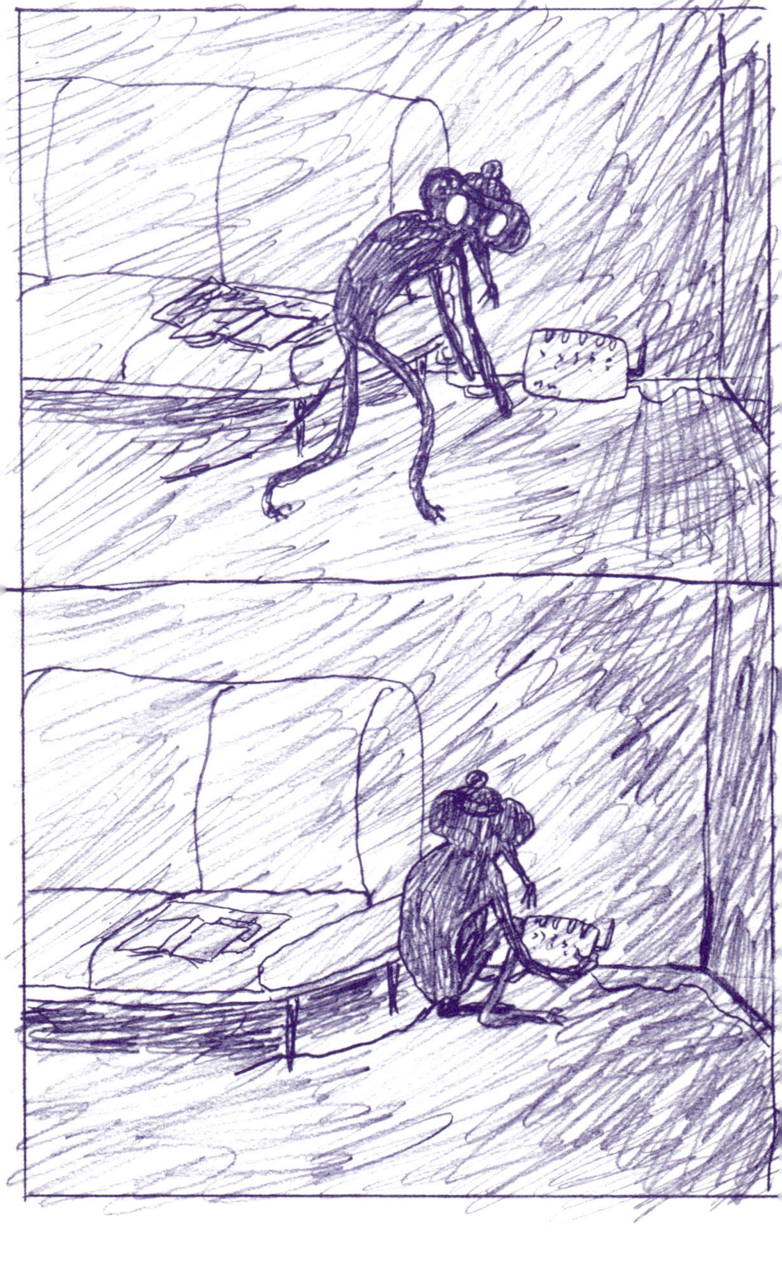

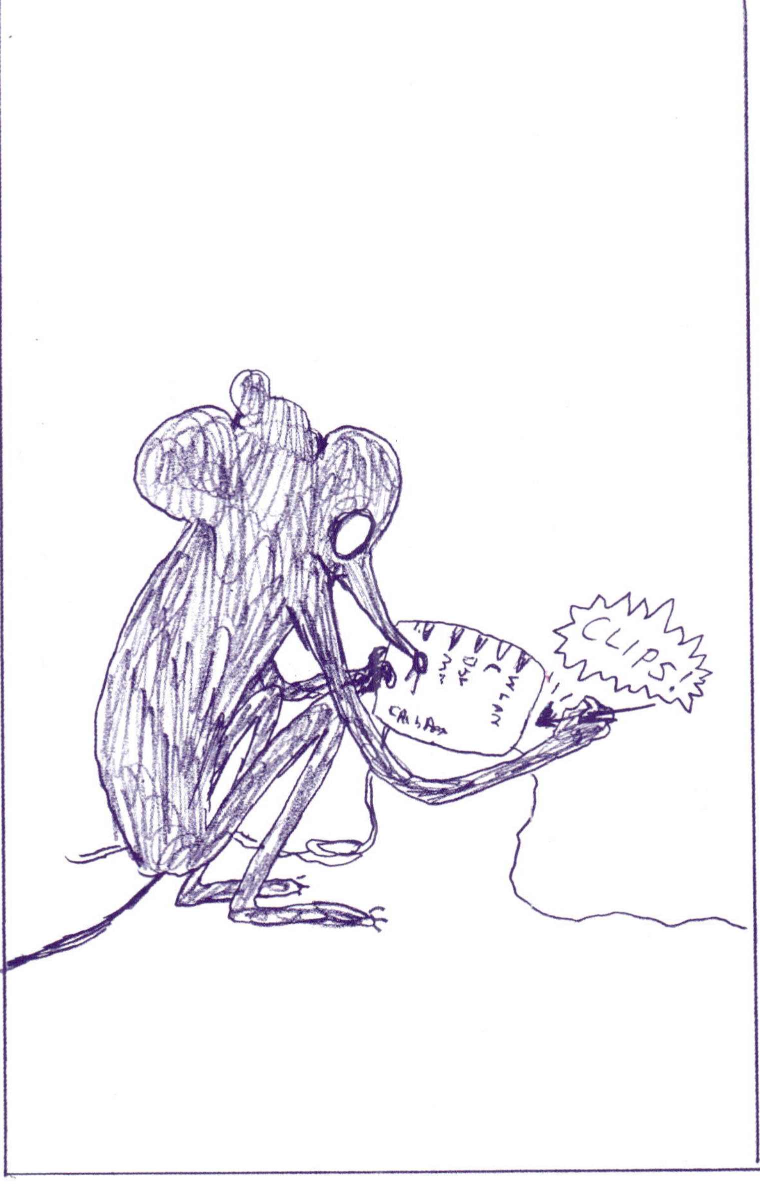
WLAN
C
DSL
3G
CALL App
CLIPS!

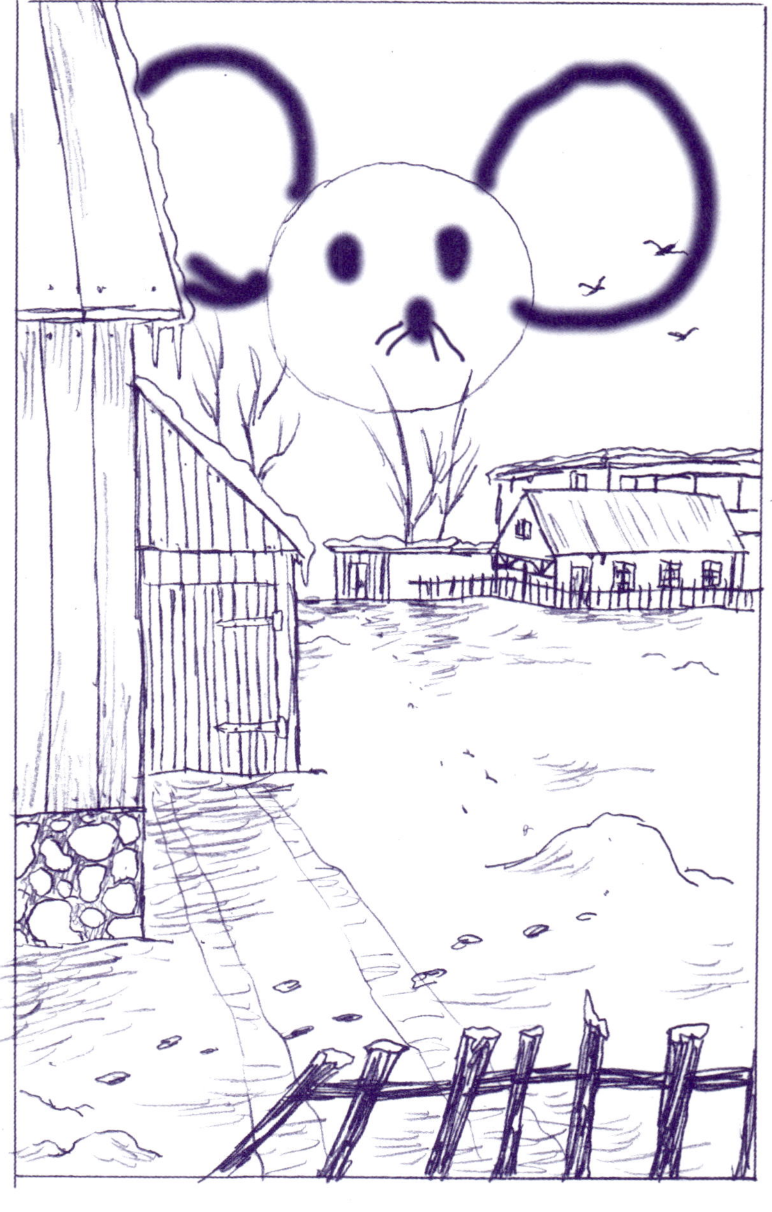

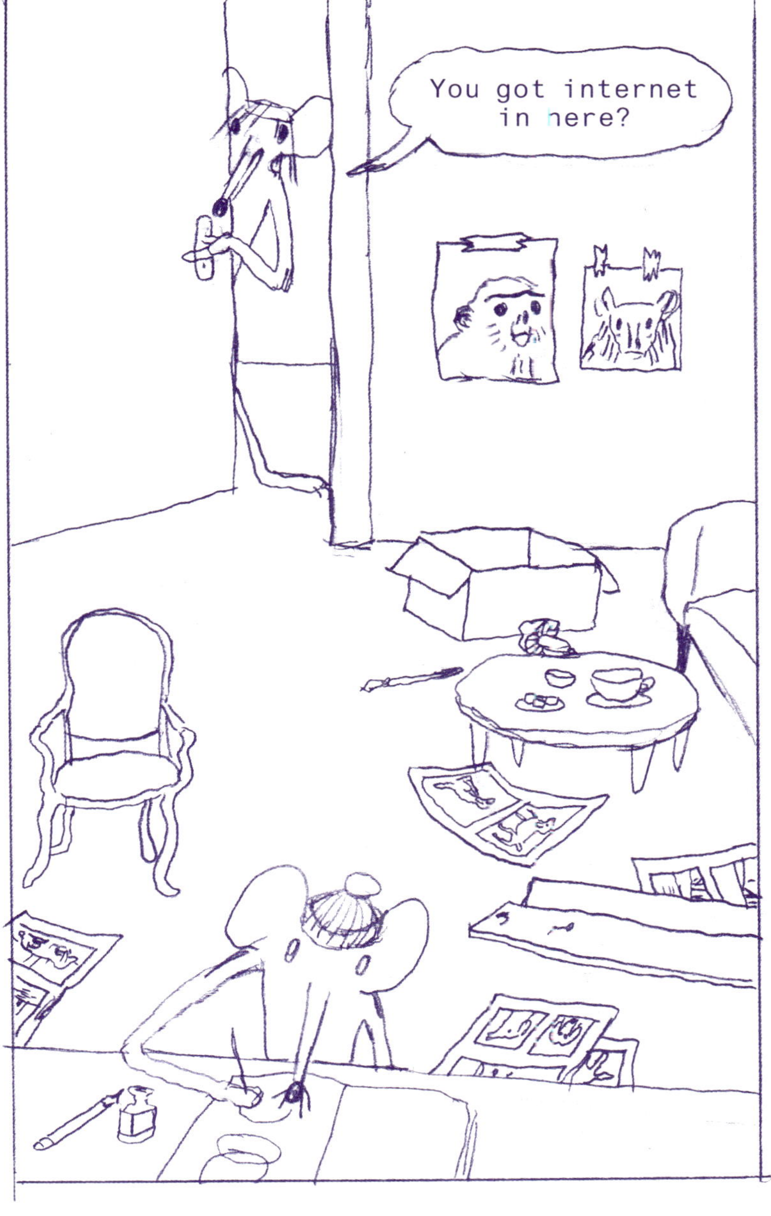

You got internet
in here?

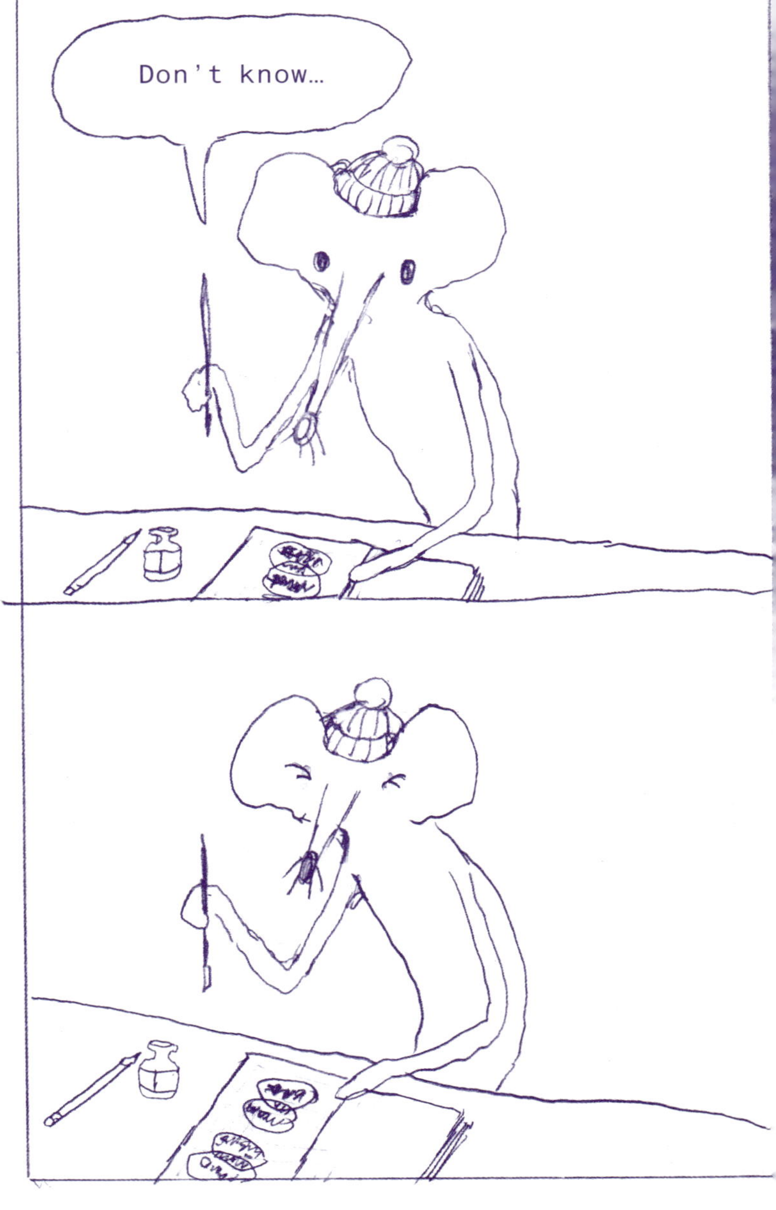

Don't know...

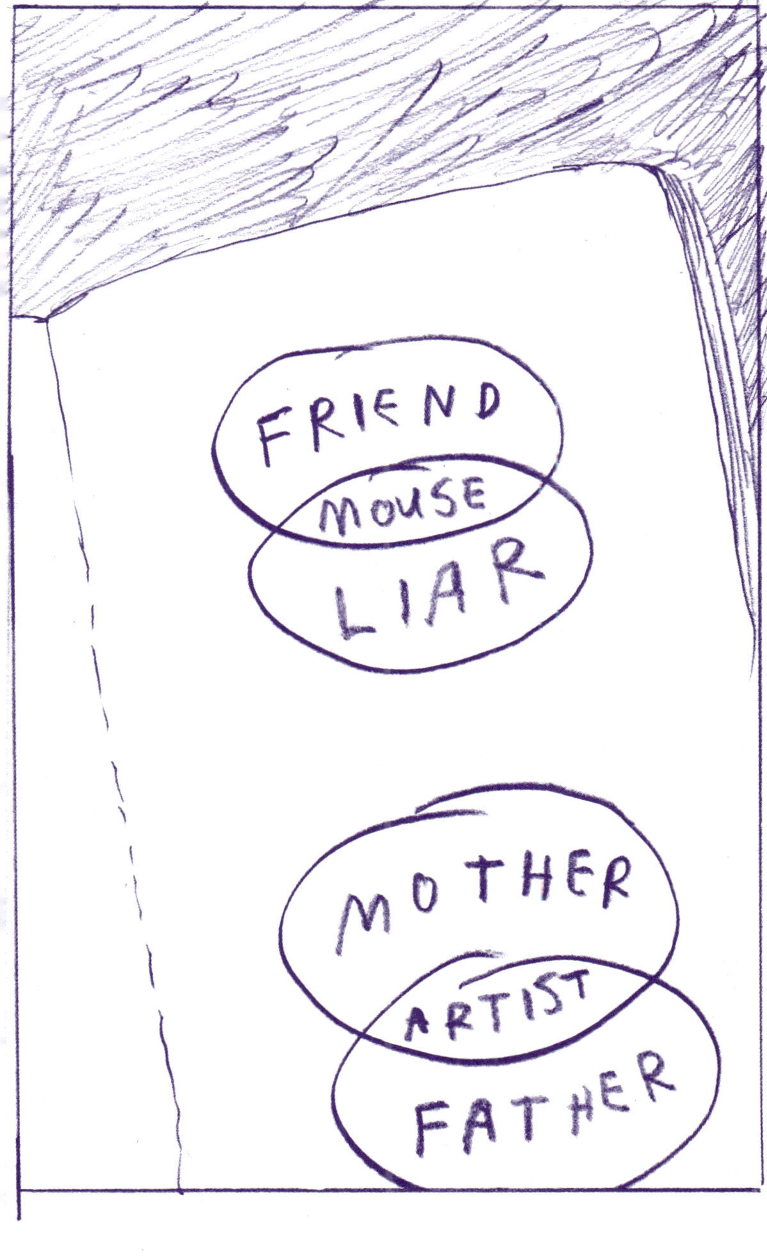

FRIEND
MOUSE
LIAR
MOTHER
ARTIST
FATHER

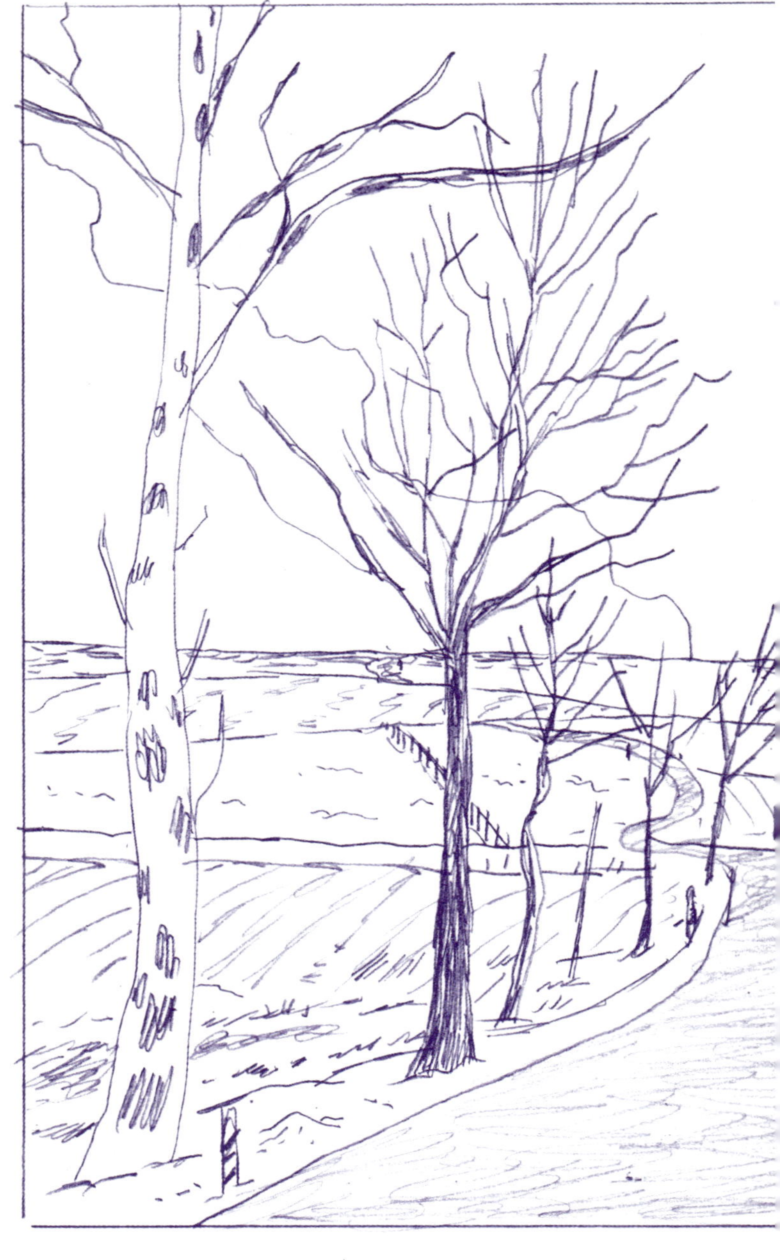

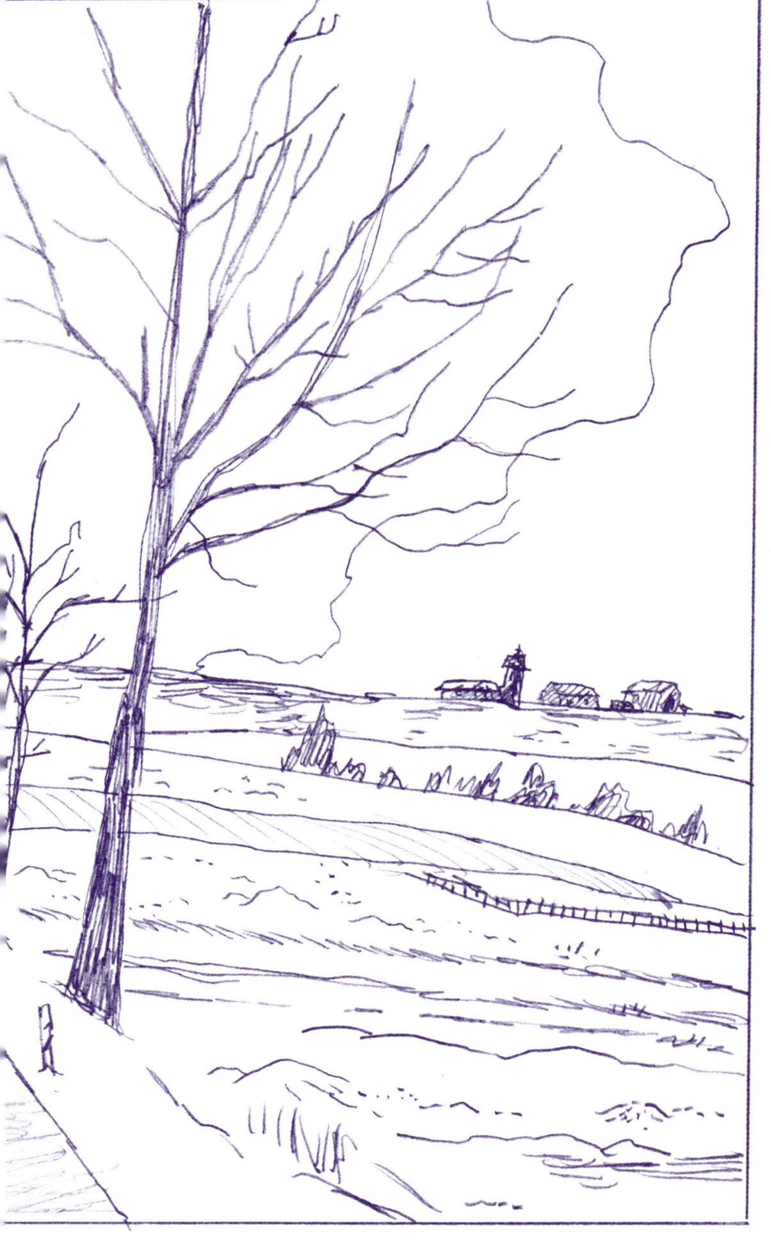

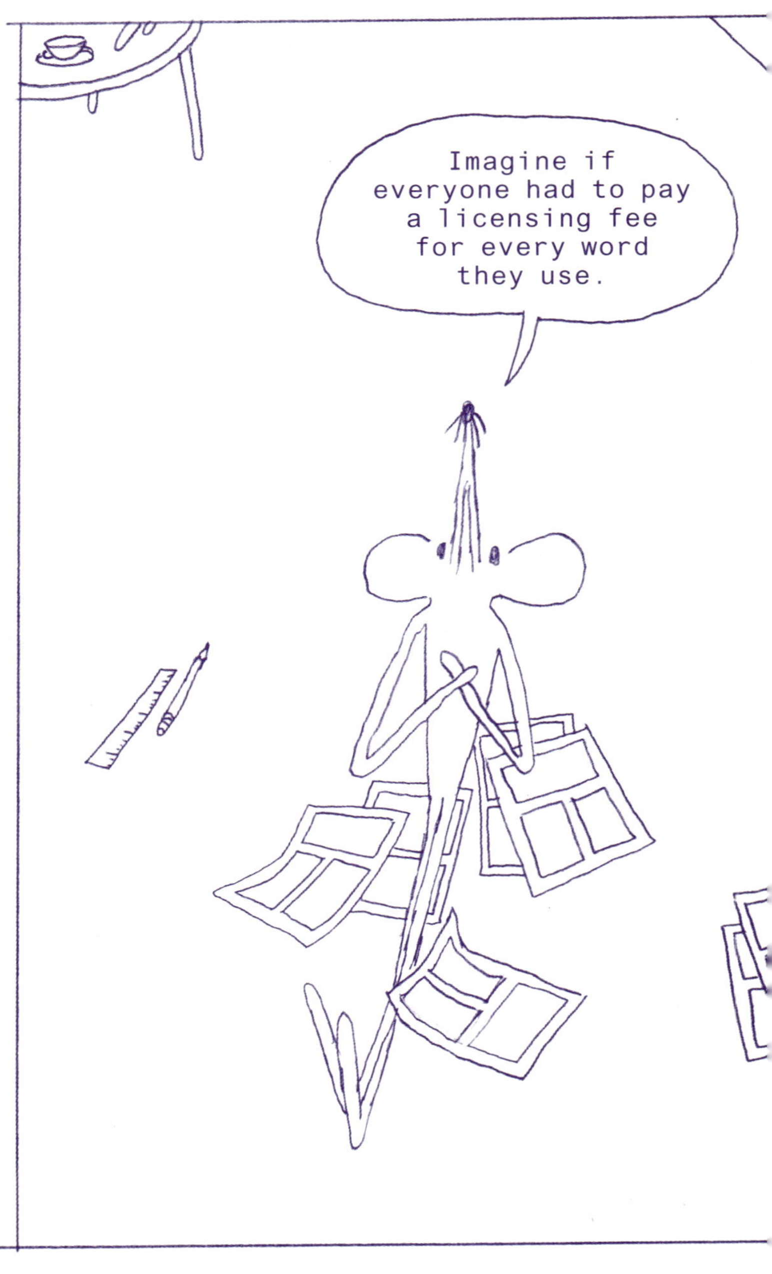

Imagine if
everyone had to pay
a licensing fee
for every word
they use.

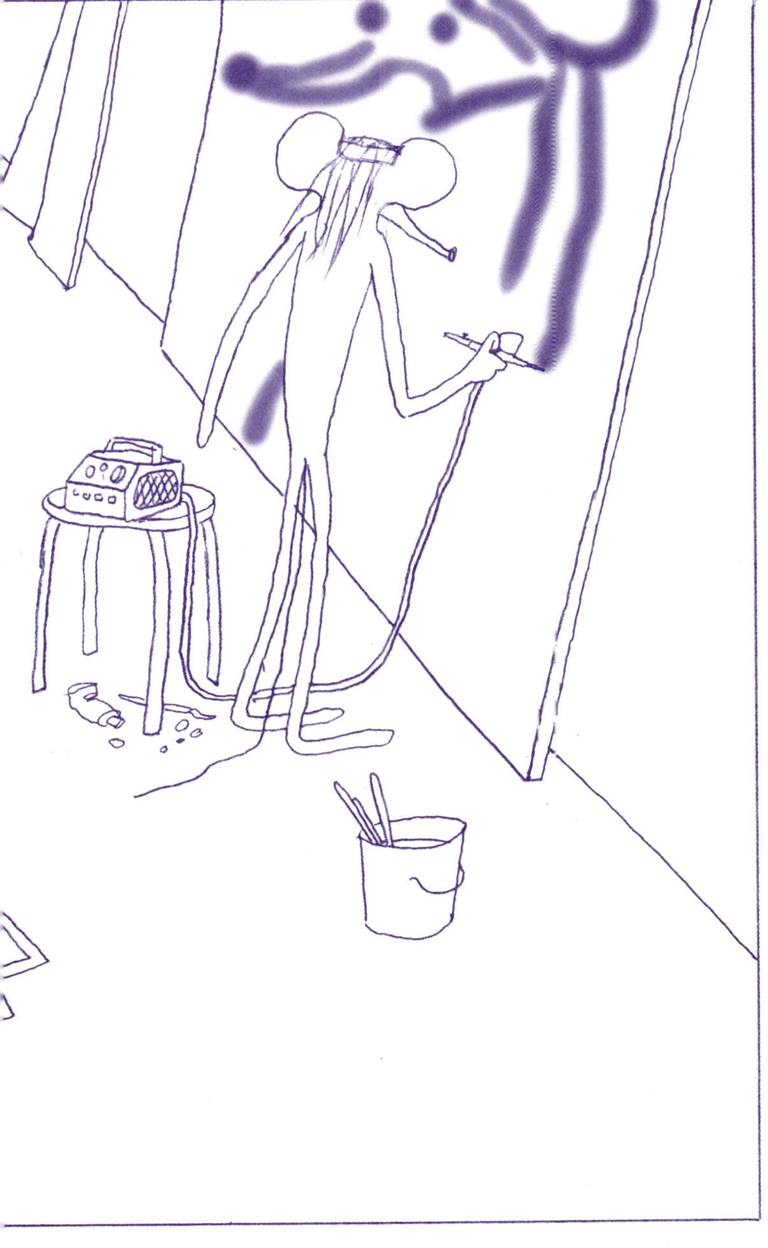

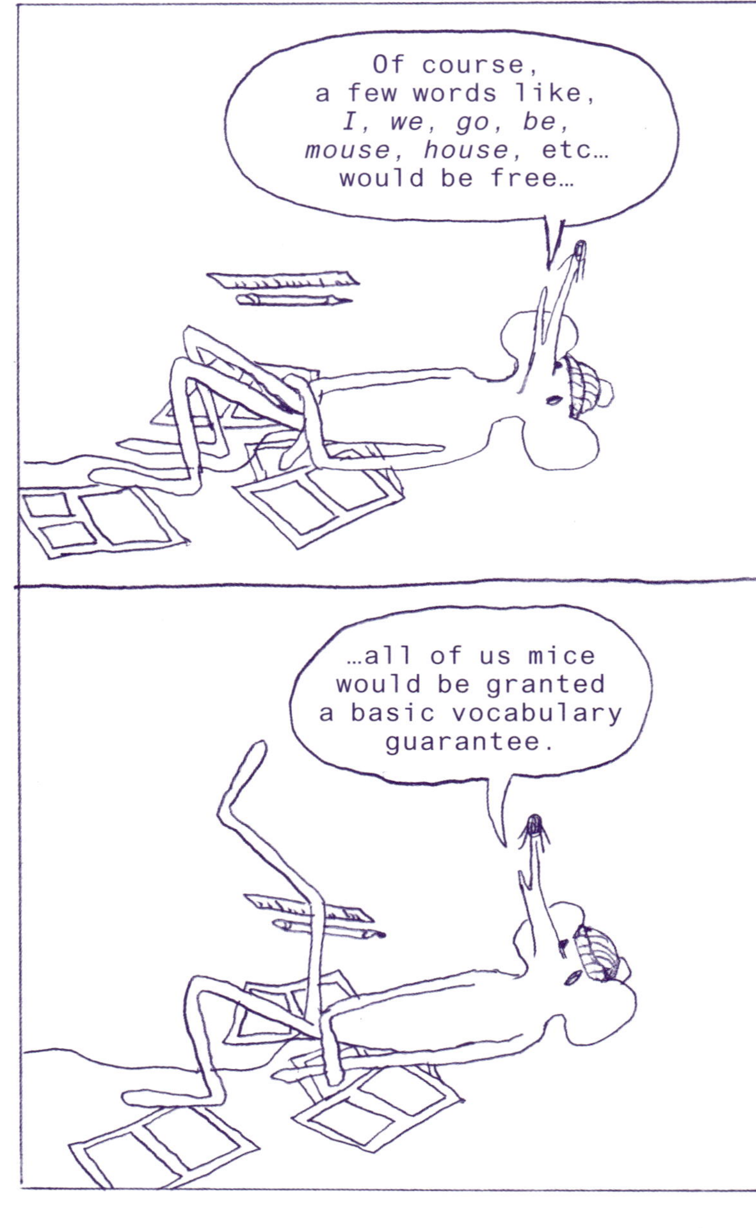
Of course,
a few words like,
I, we, go, be,
mouse, house, etc…
would be free…

…all of us mice
would be granted
a basic vocabulary
guarantee.

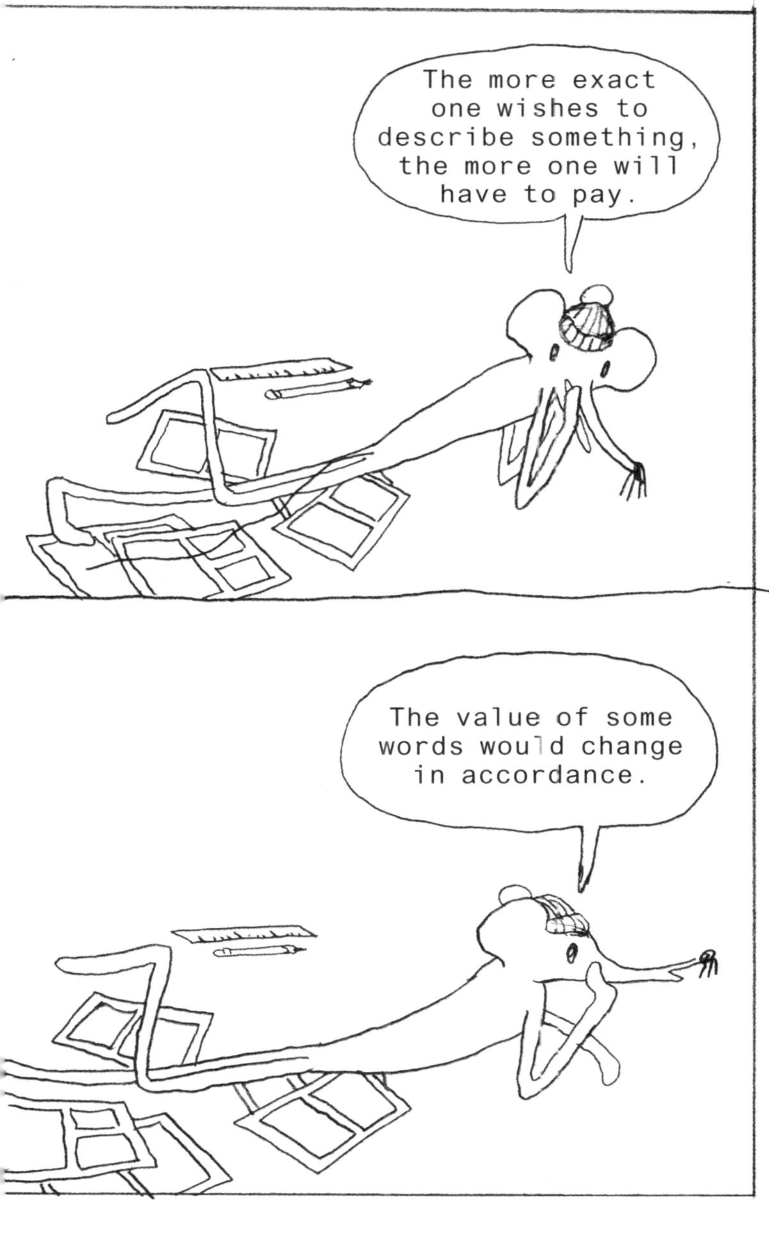
The more exact
one wishes to
describe something,
the more one will
have to pay.
The value of some
words would change
in accordance.

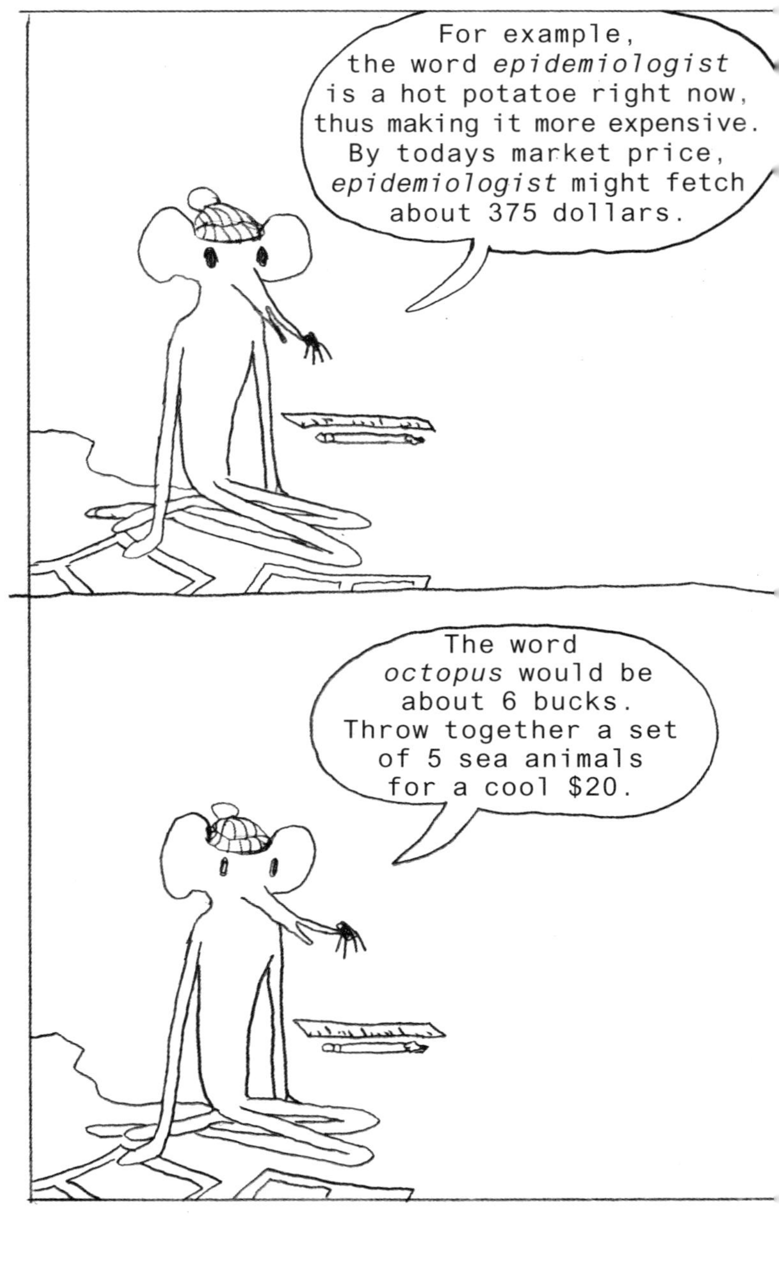

For example, the word epidemiologist is a hot potatoe right now, thus making it more expensive. By todays market price, epidemiologist might fetch about 375 dollars.
The word octopus would be about 6 bucks. Throw together a set of 5 sea animals for a cool $20.

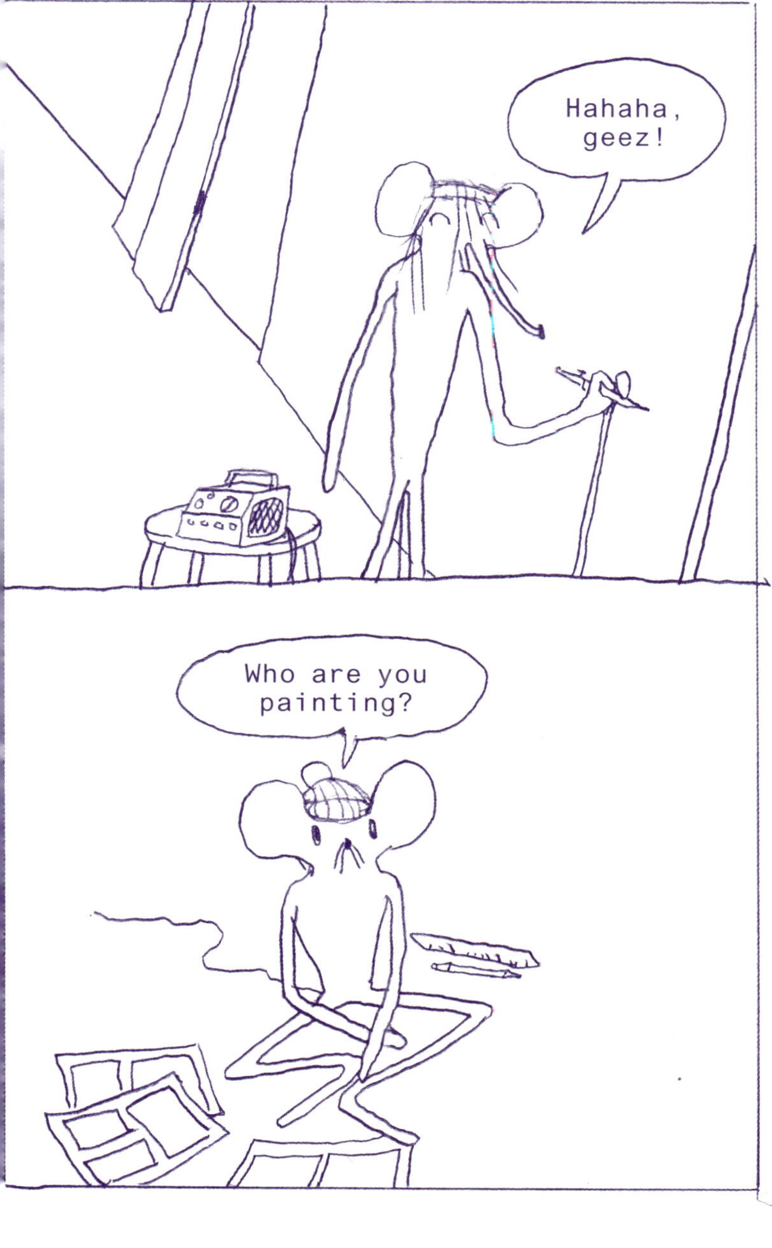

Hahaha, geez!
Who are you painting?

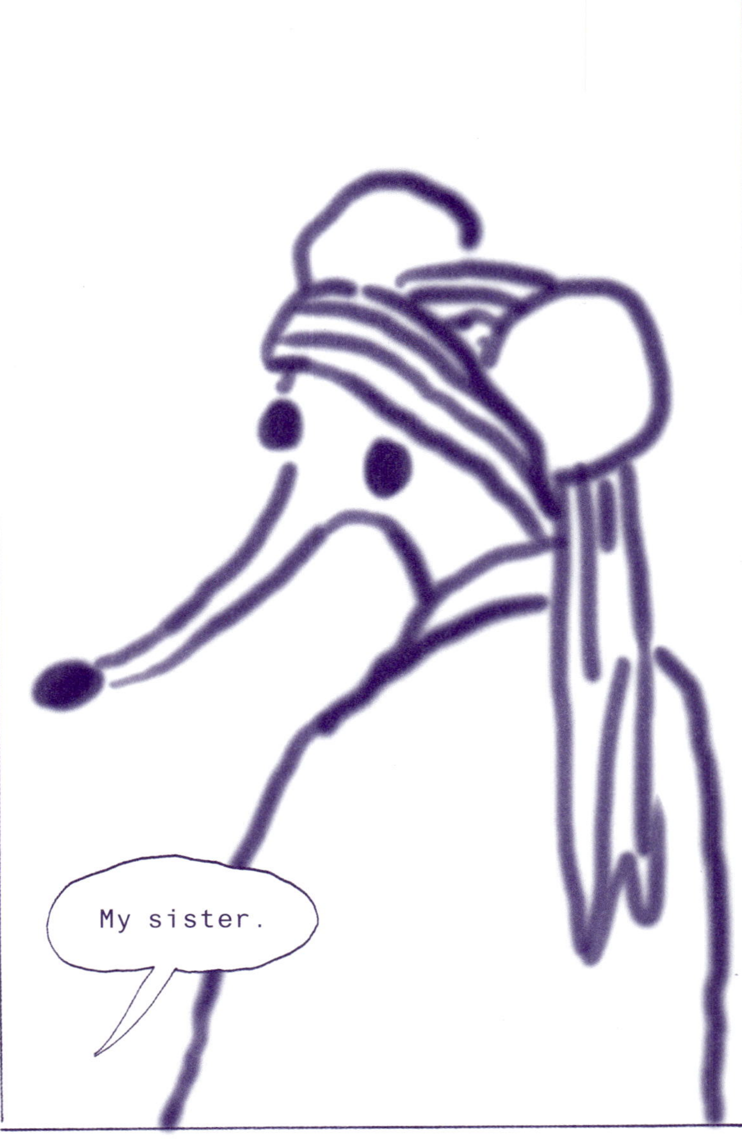
My sister.

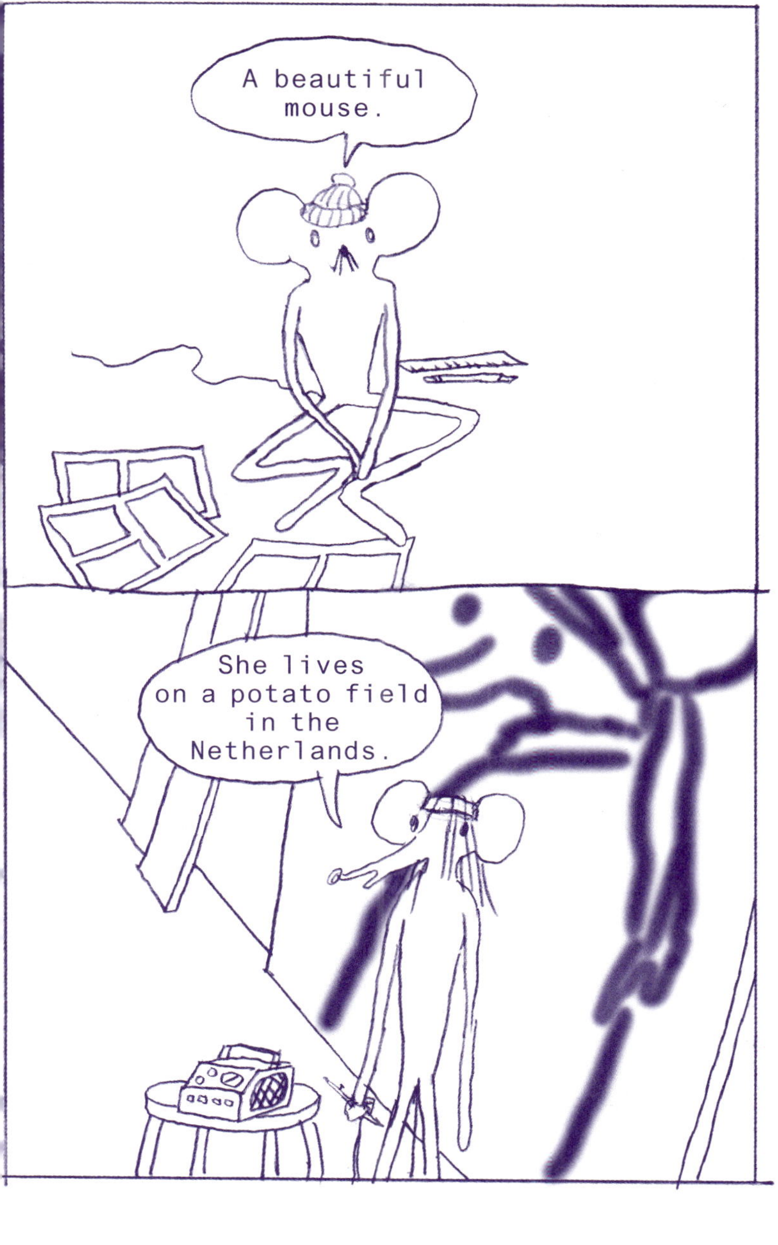

A beautiful mouse.
She lives on a potato field in the Netherlands.

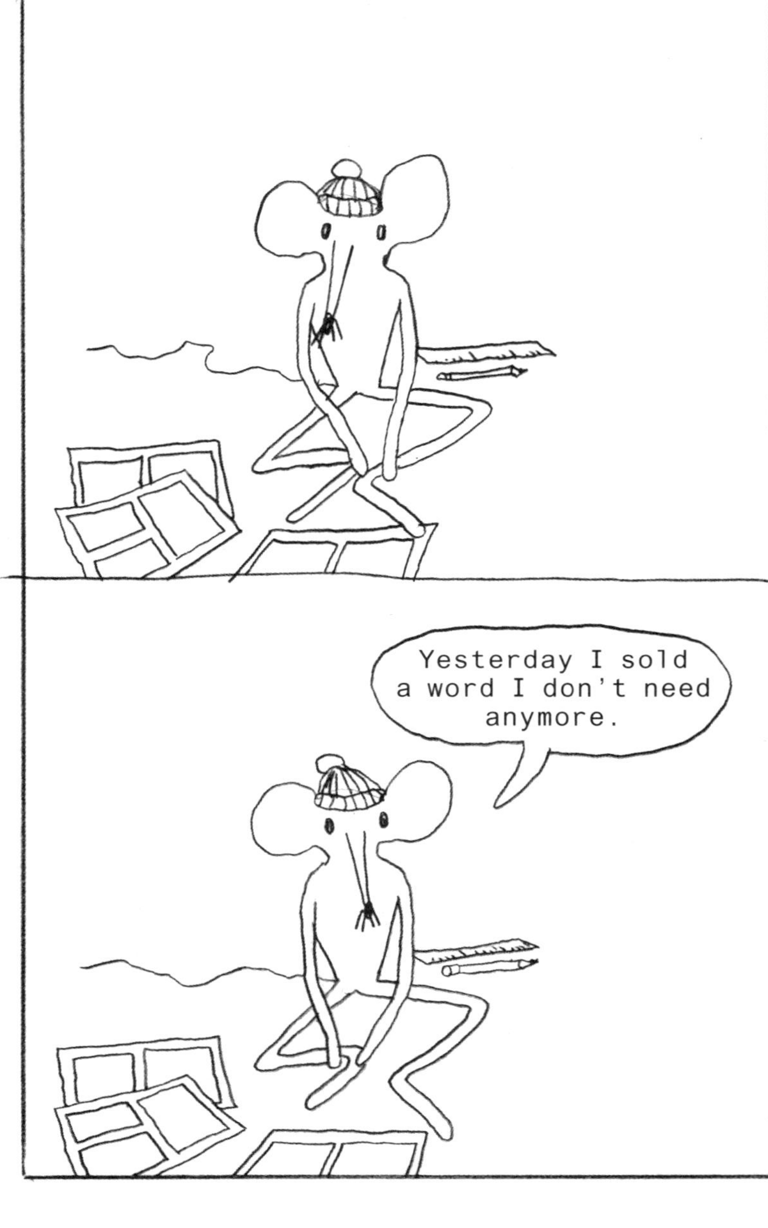
Yesterday I sold
a word I don't need
anymore.

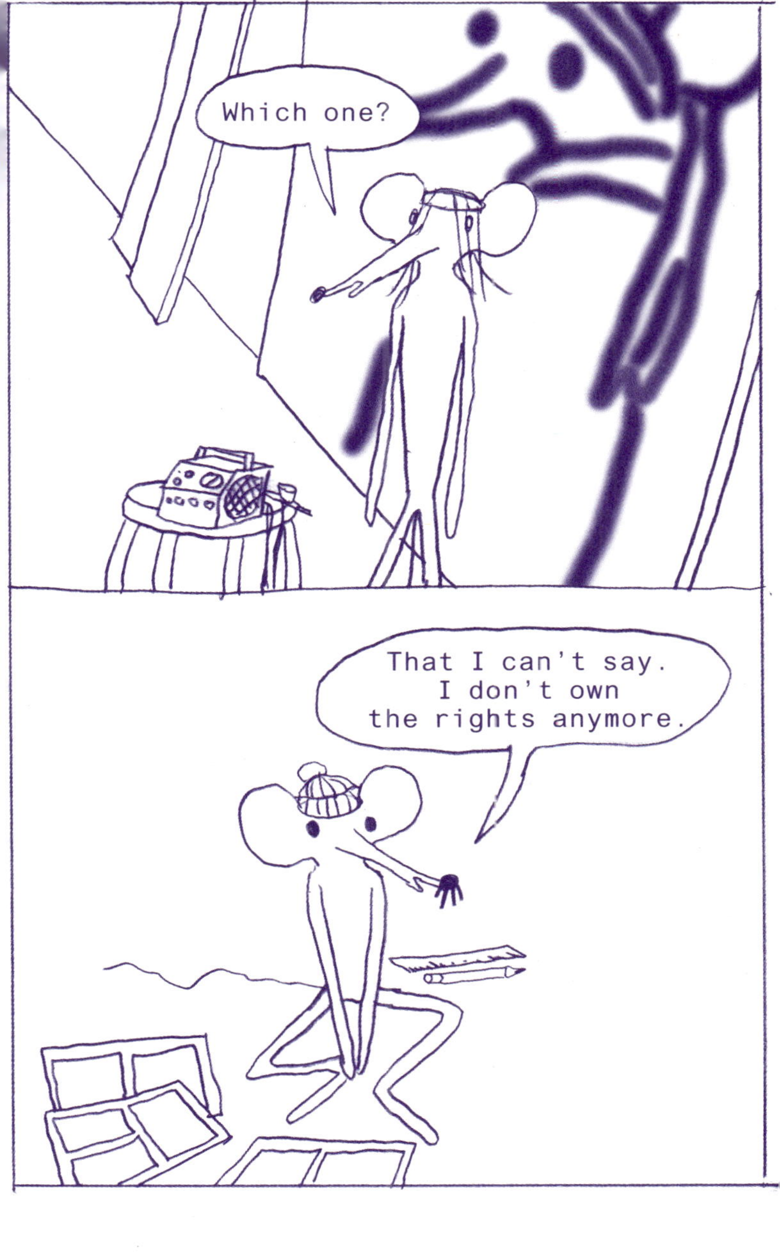
Which one?
That I can't say.
I don't own
the rights anymore.

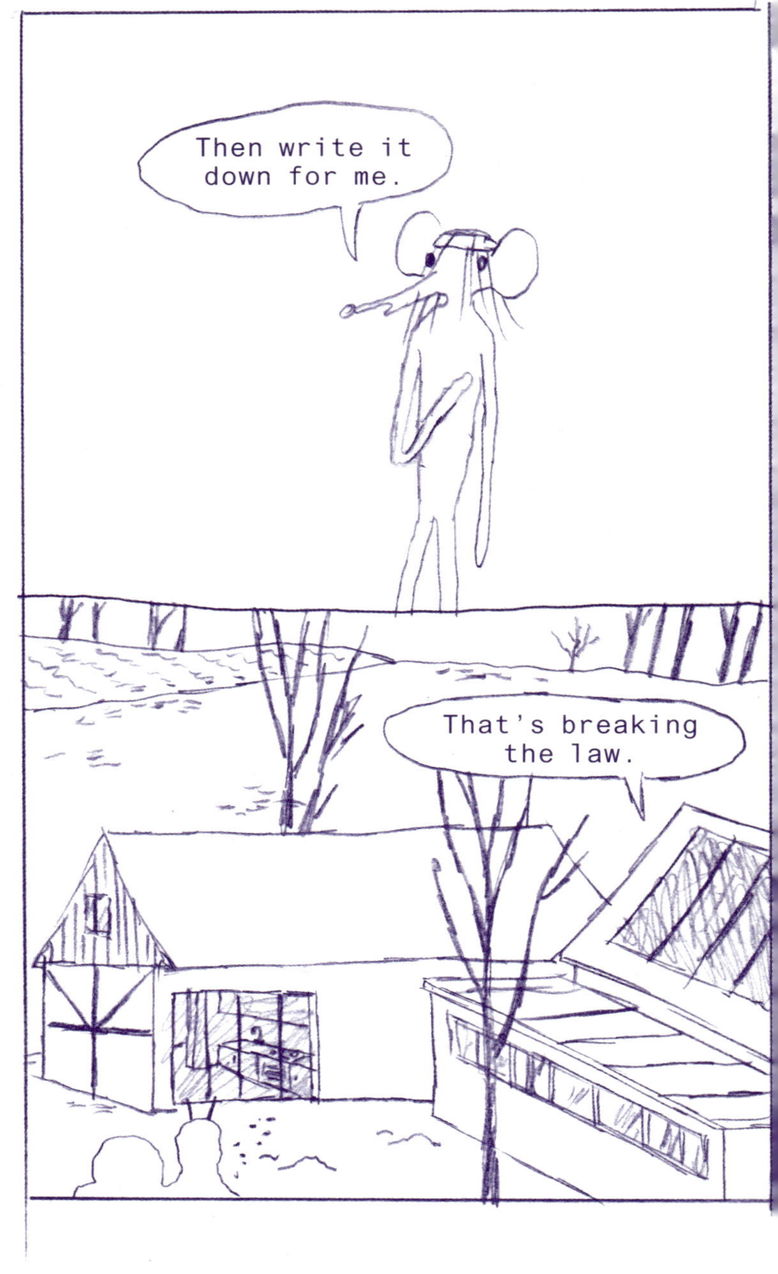

Then write it
down for me.

That's breaking
the law.

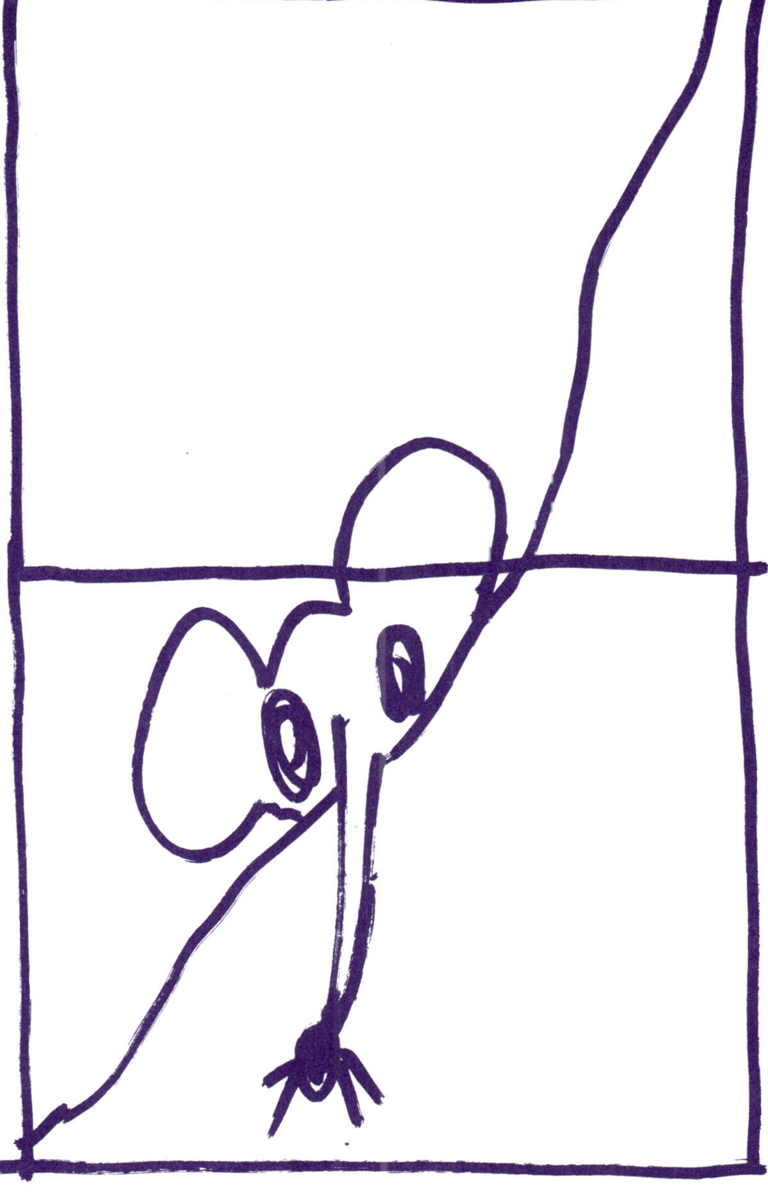

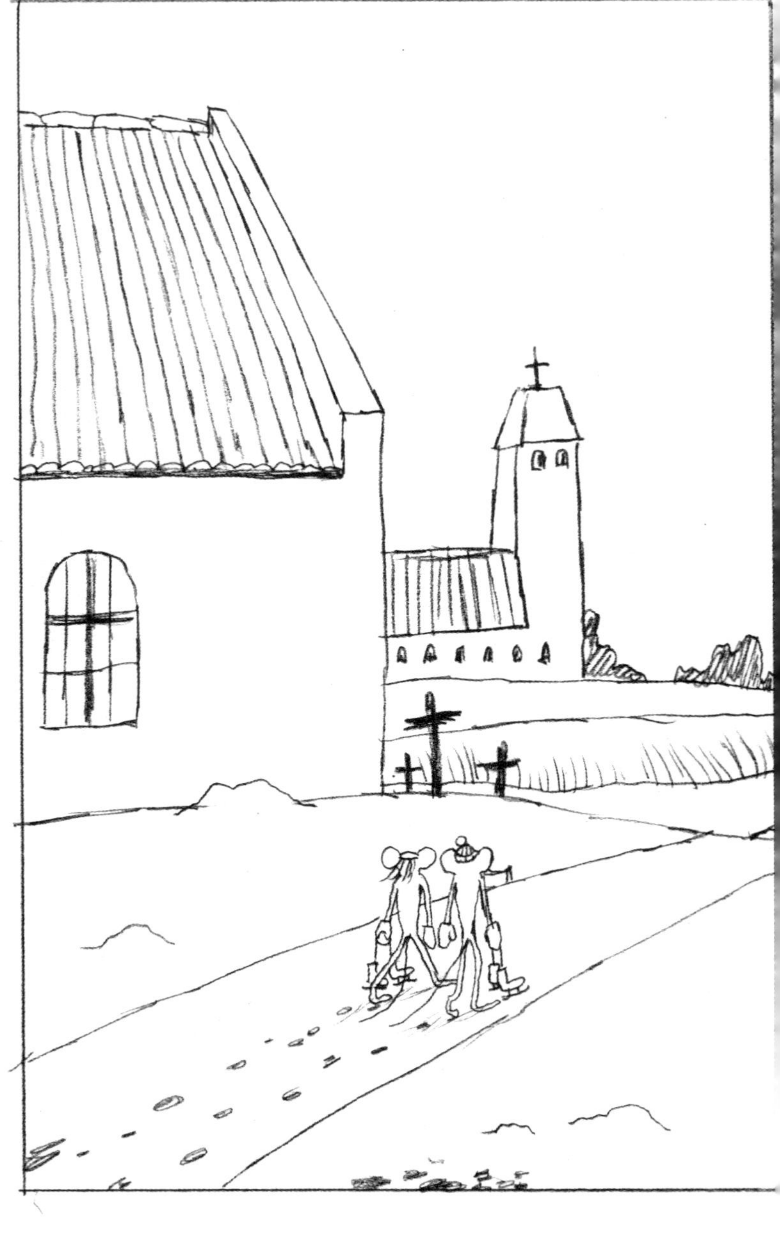

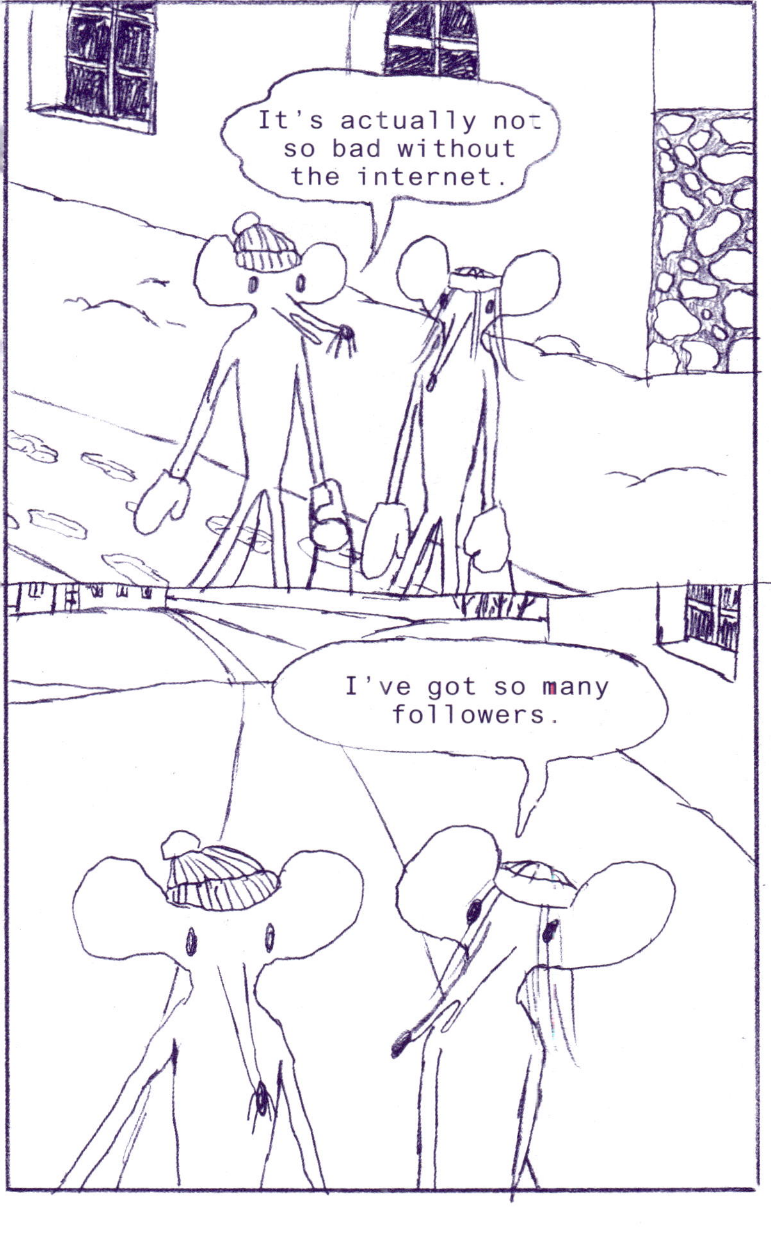

It's actually not so bad without the internet.
I've got so many followers.

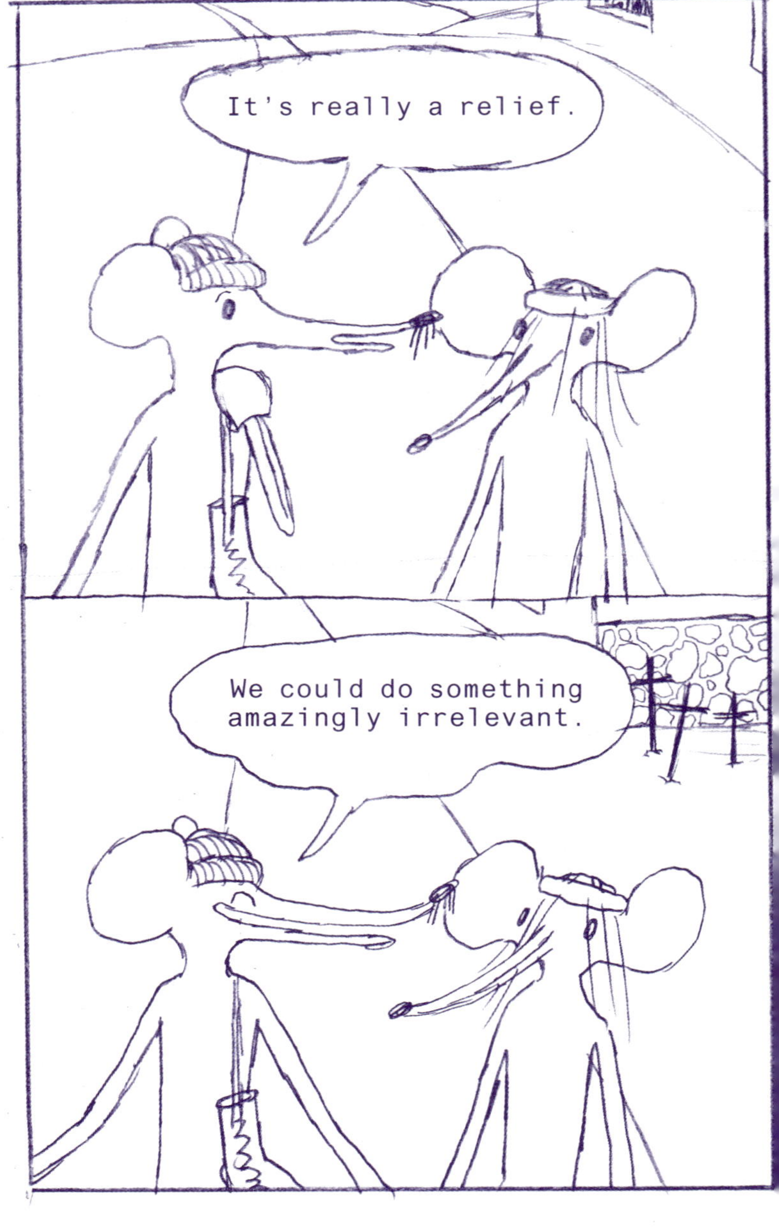

It's really a relief.

We could do something amazingly irrelevant.

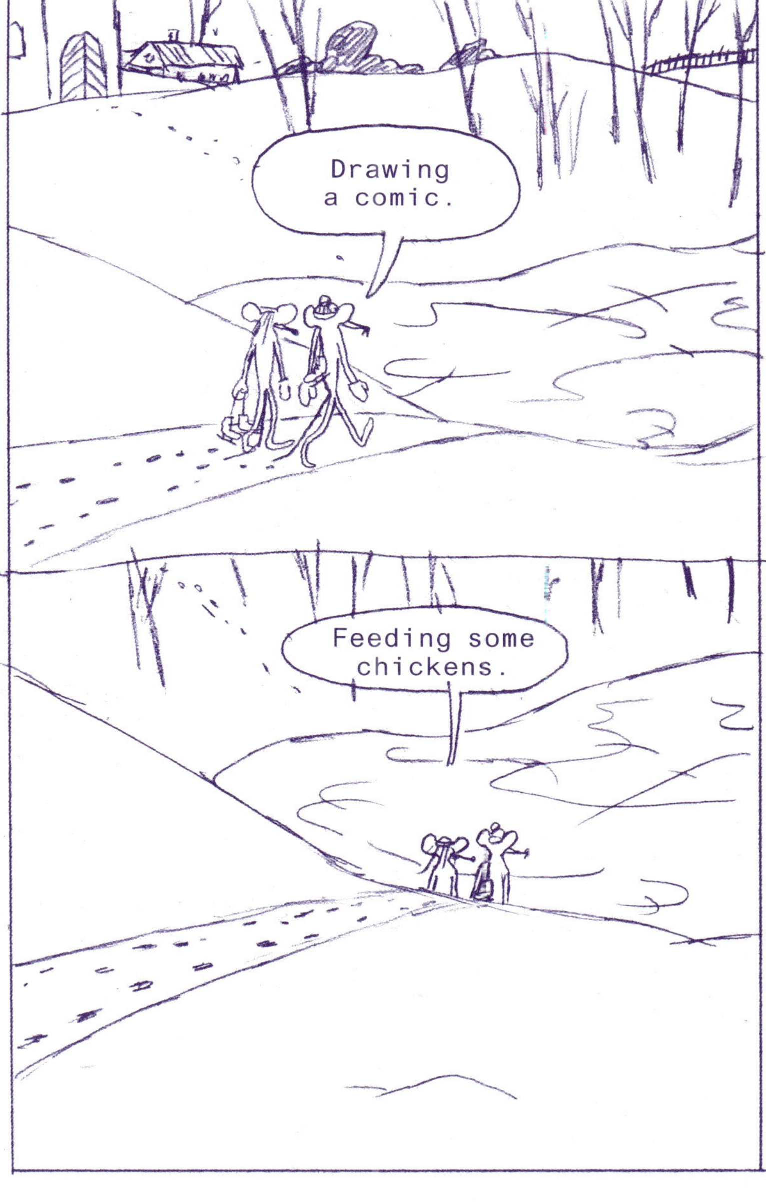

Drawing a comic.
Feeding some chickens.

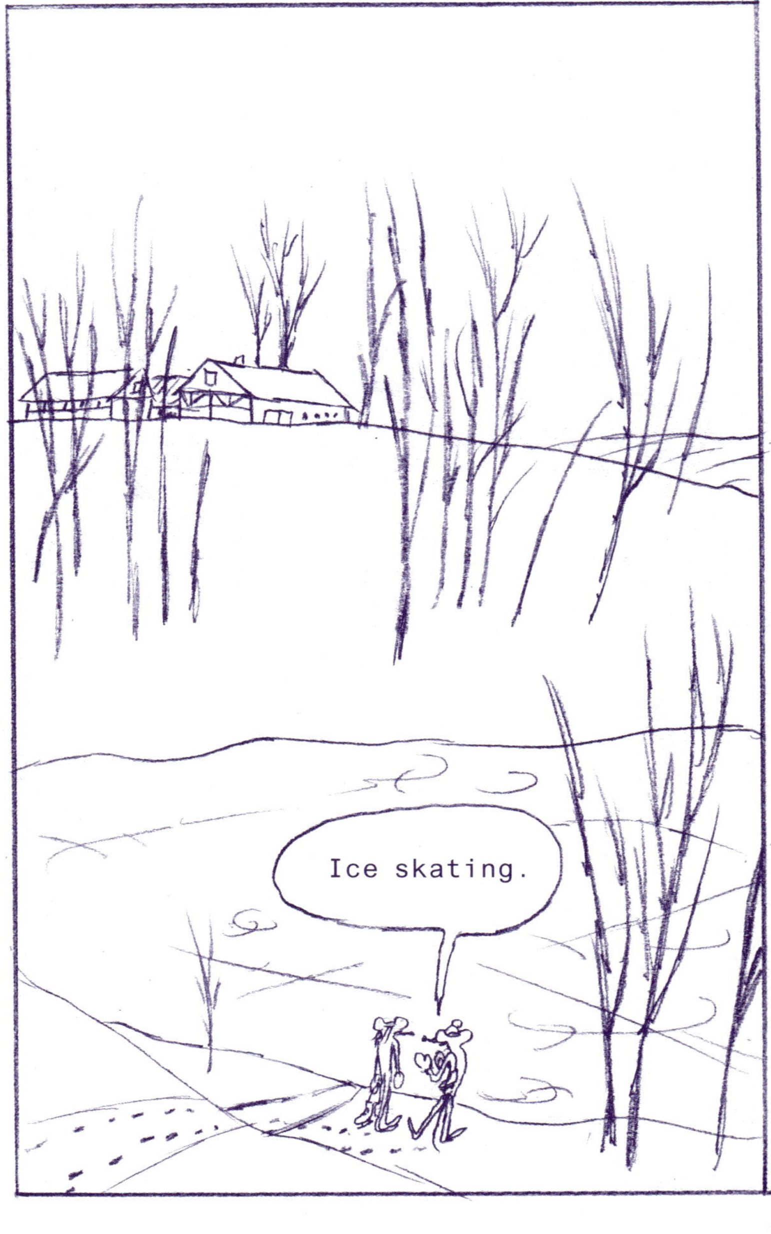

Ice skating.

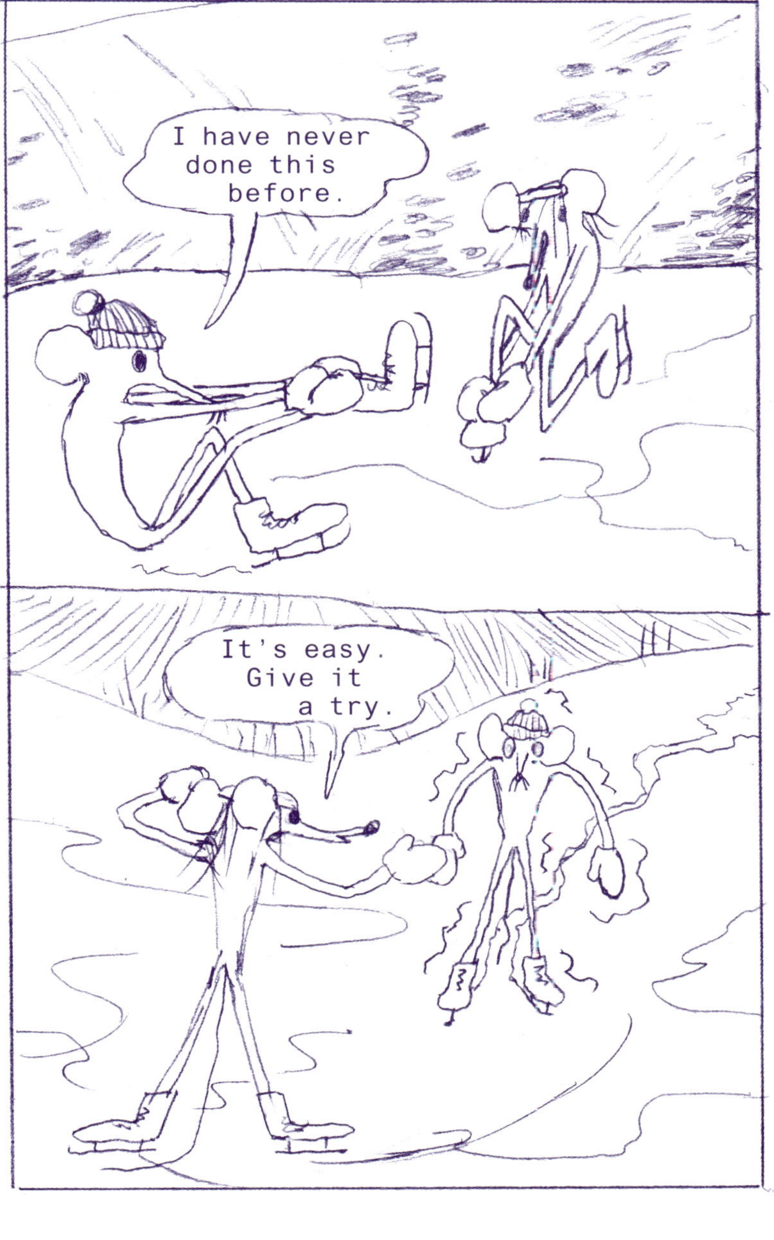

I have never
done this
before.

It's easy.
Give it
a try.

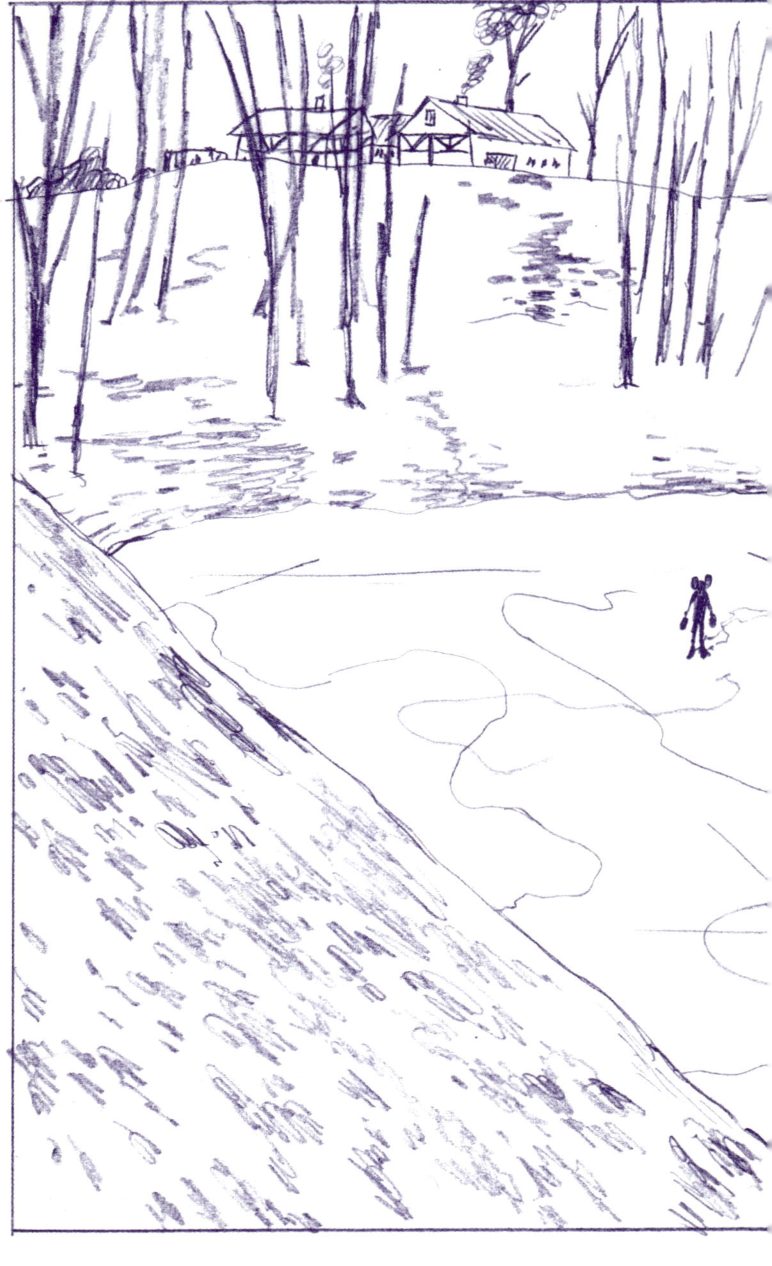

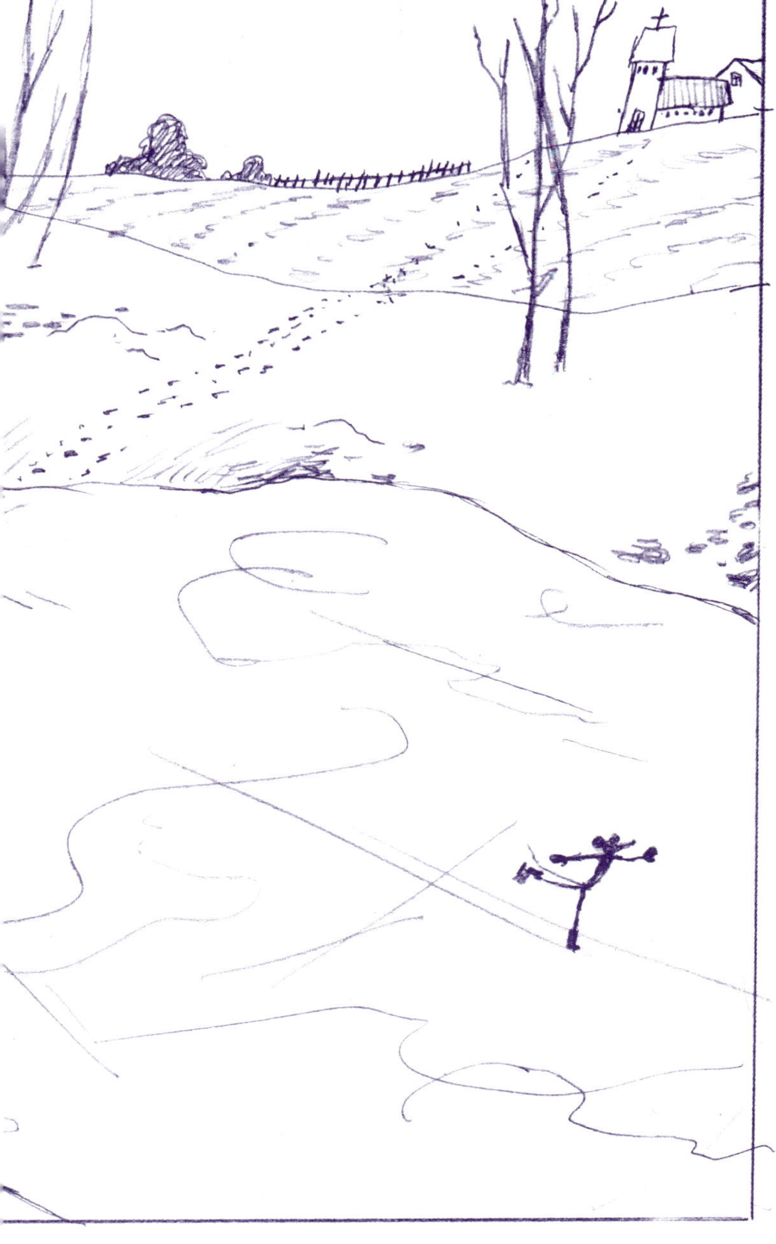

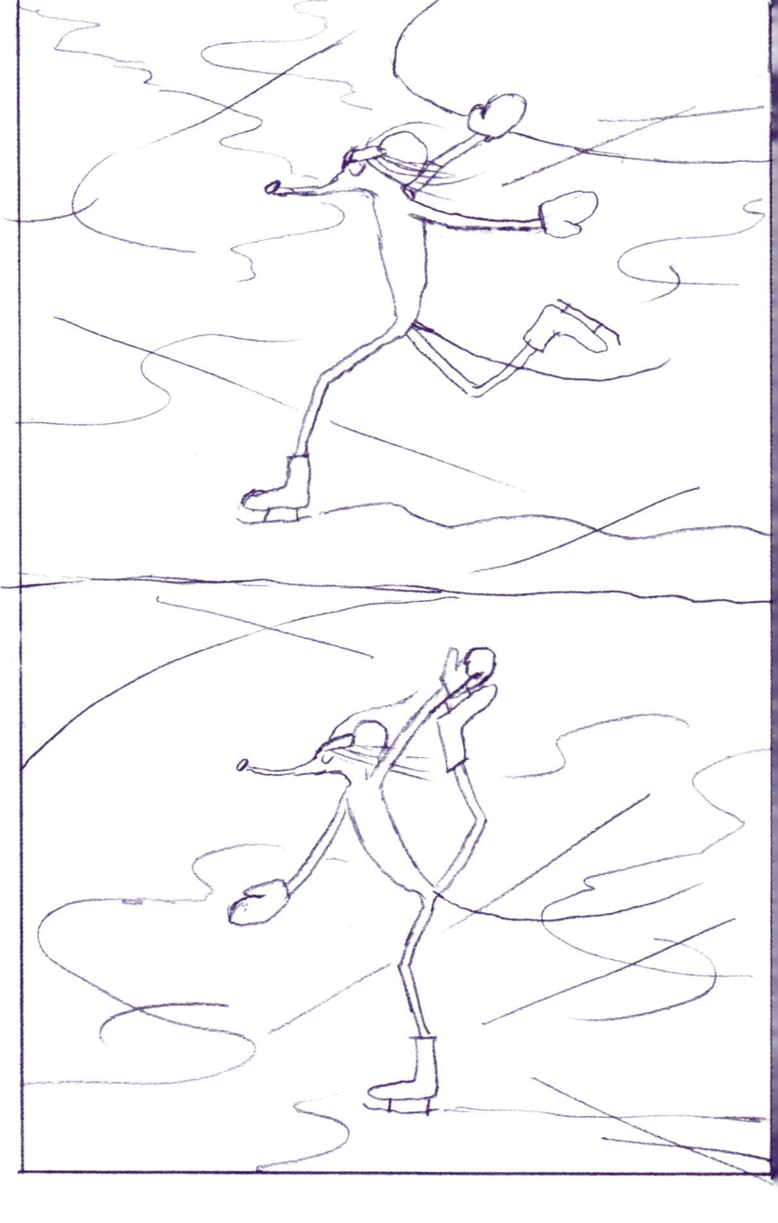

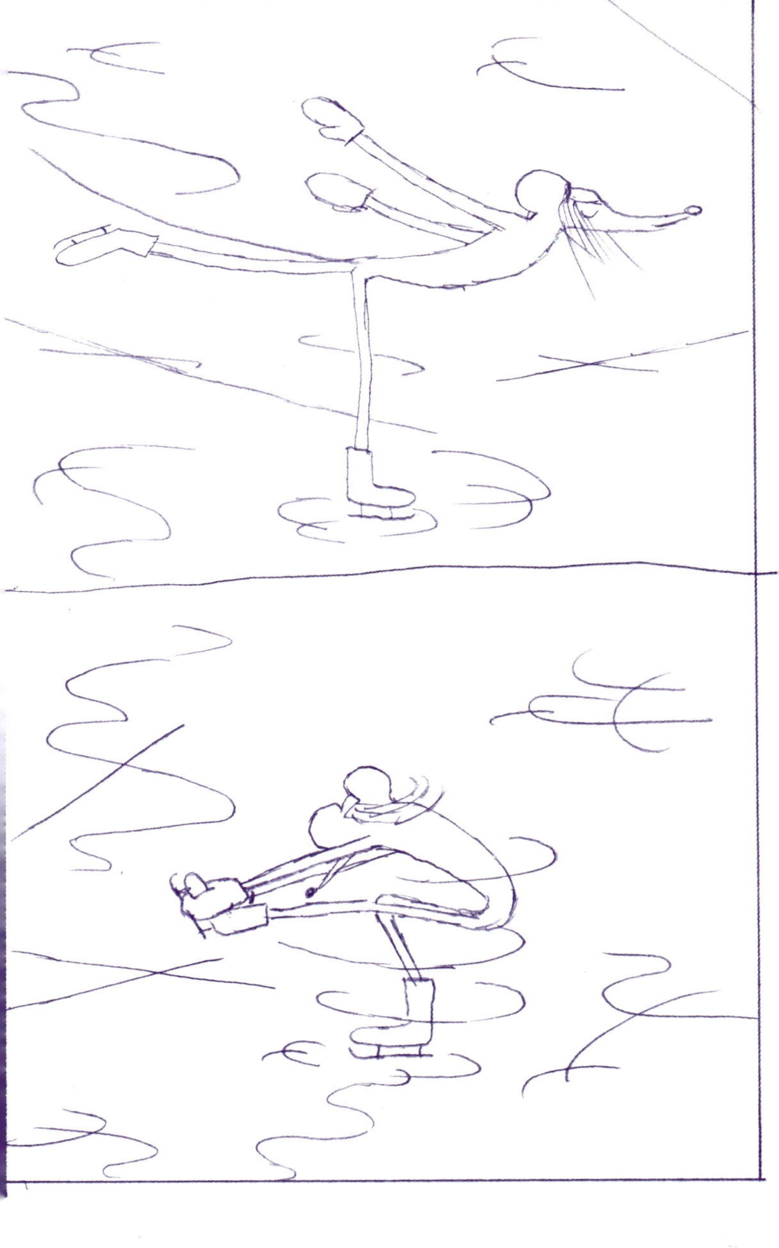

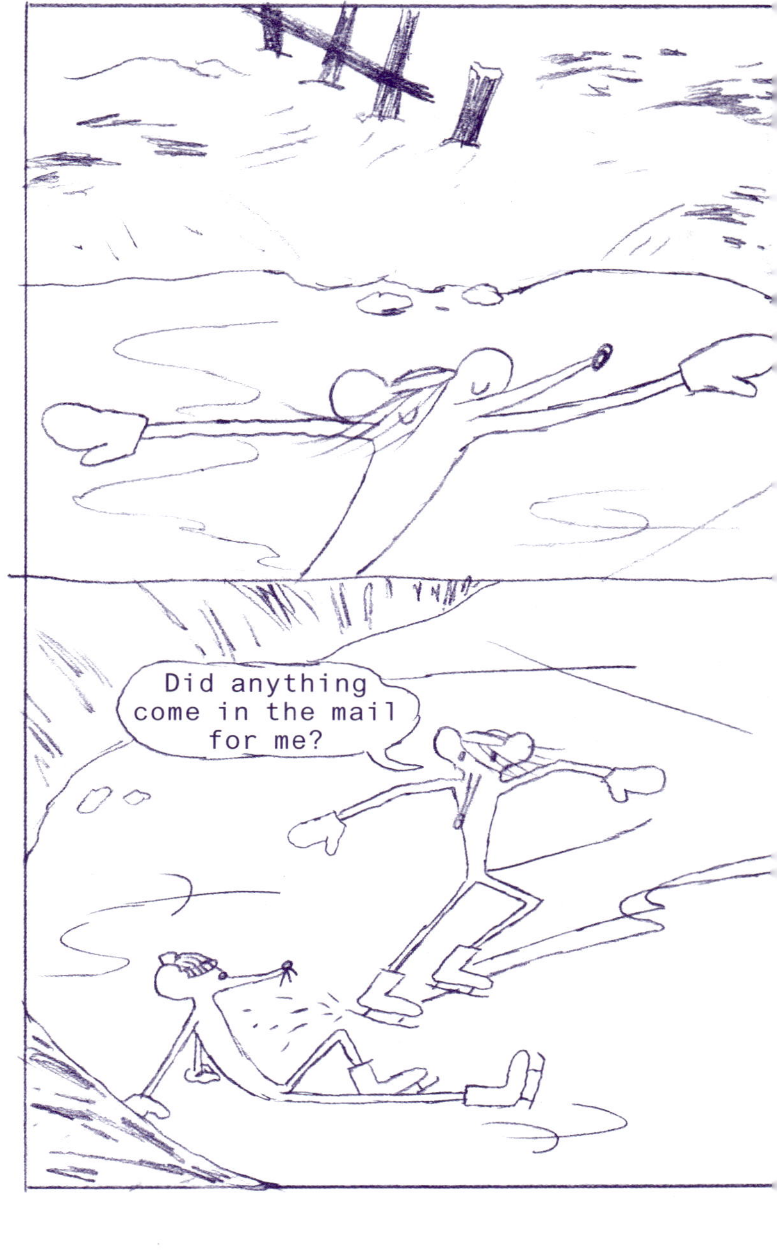

Did anything
come in the mail
for me?

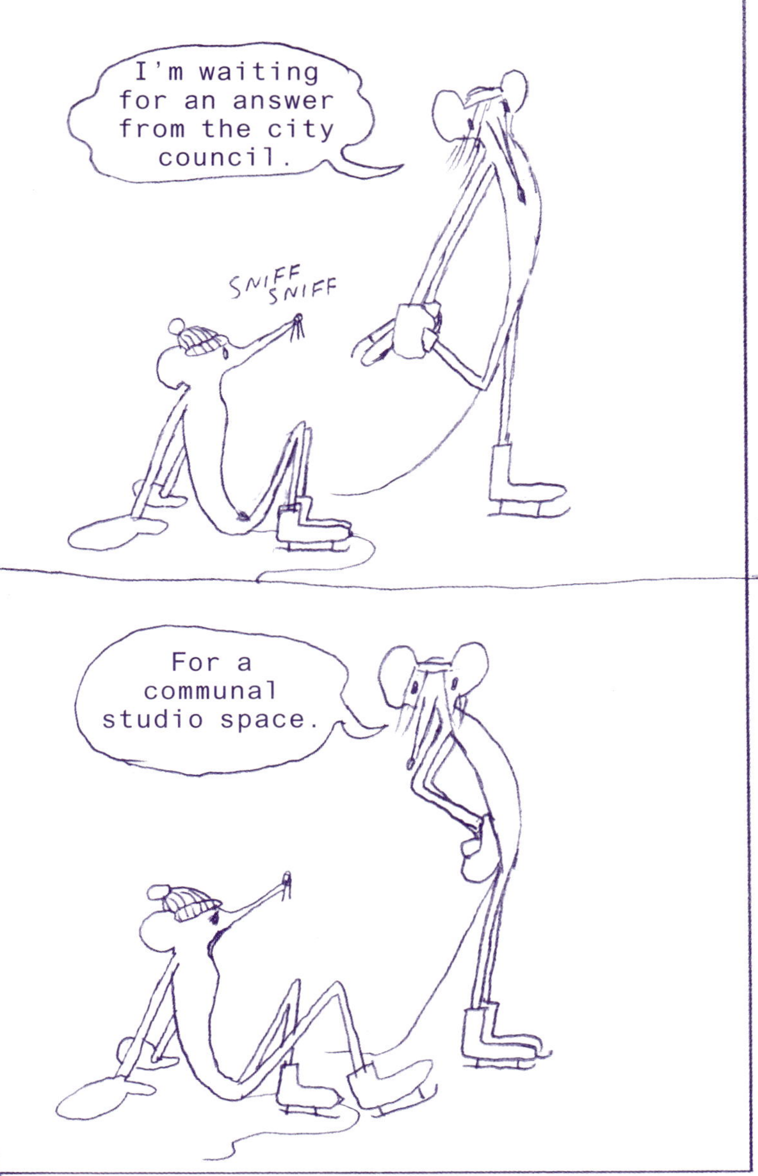

I'm waiting
for an answer
from the city
council.
SNIFF SNIFF
For a
communal
studio space.

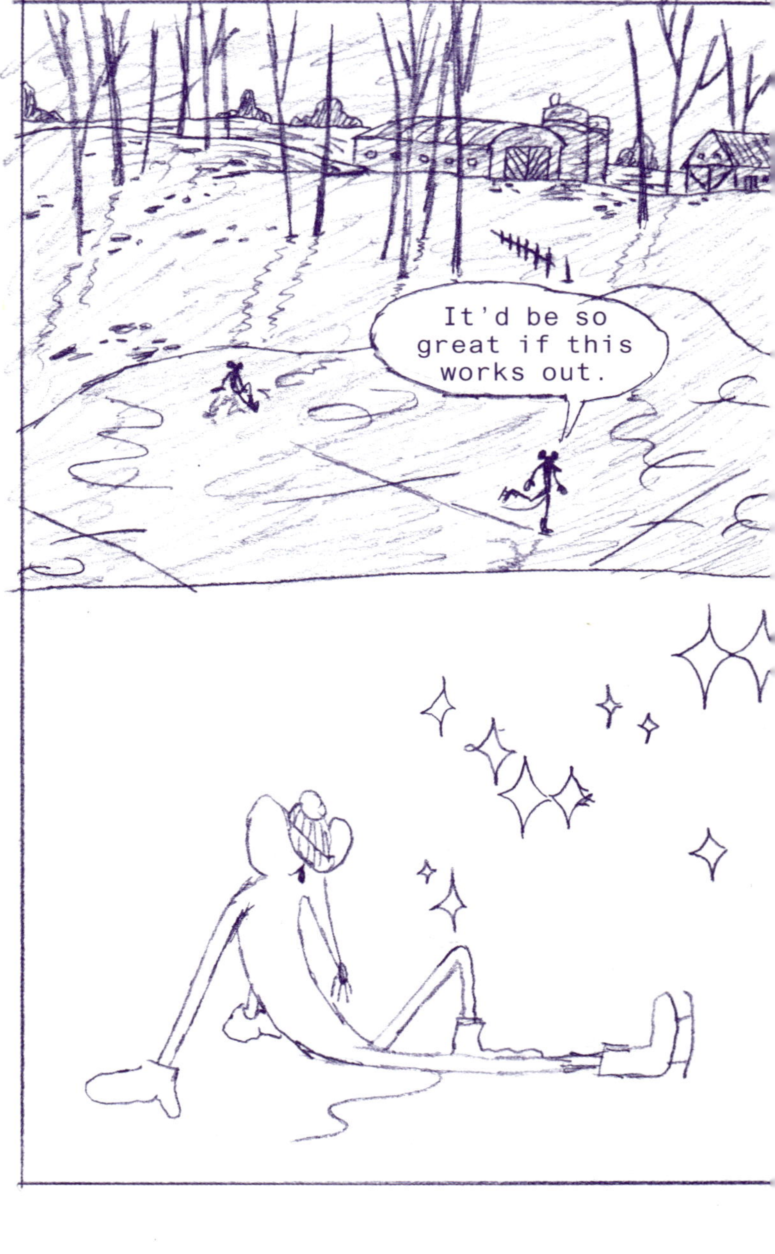

It'd be so great if this works out.

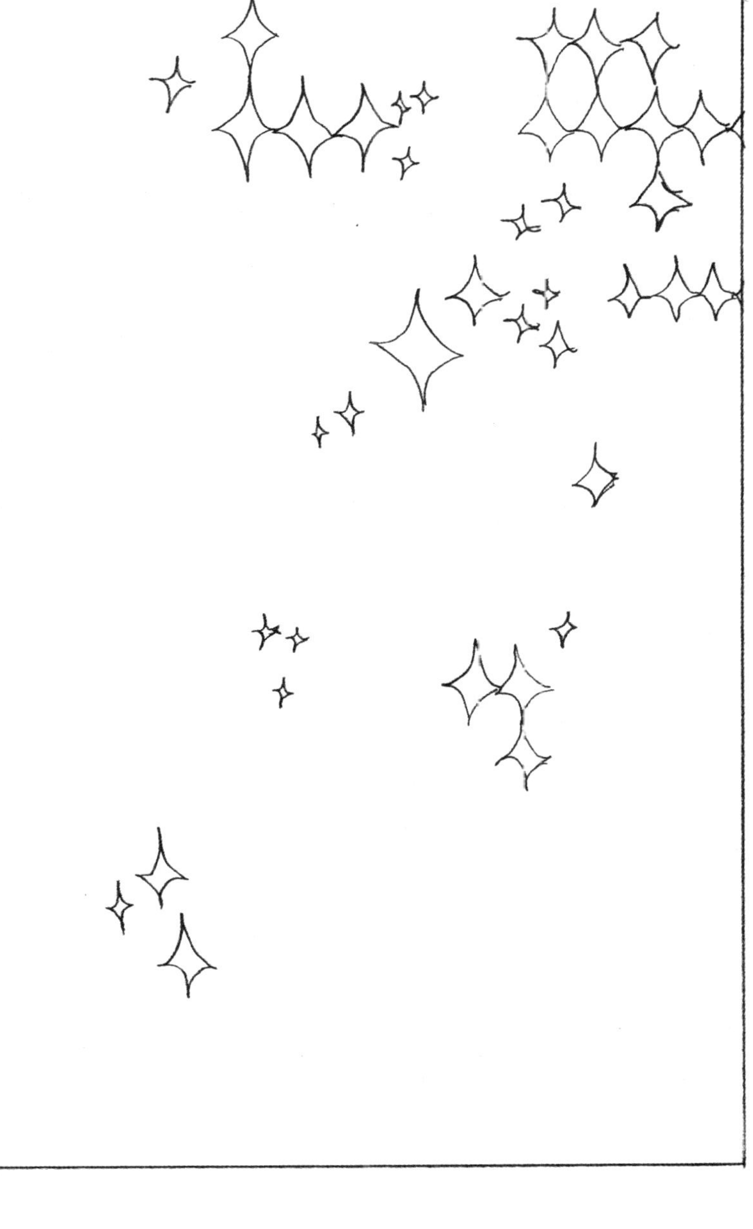

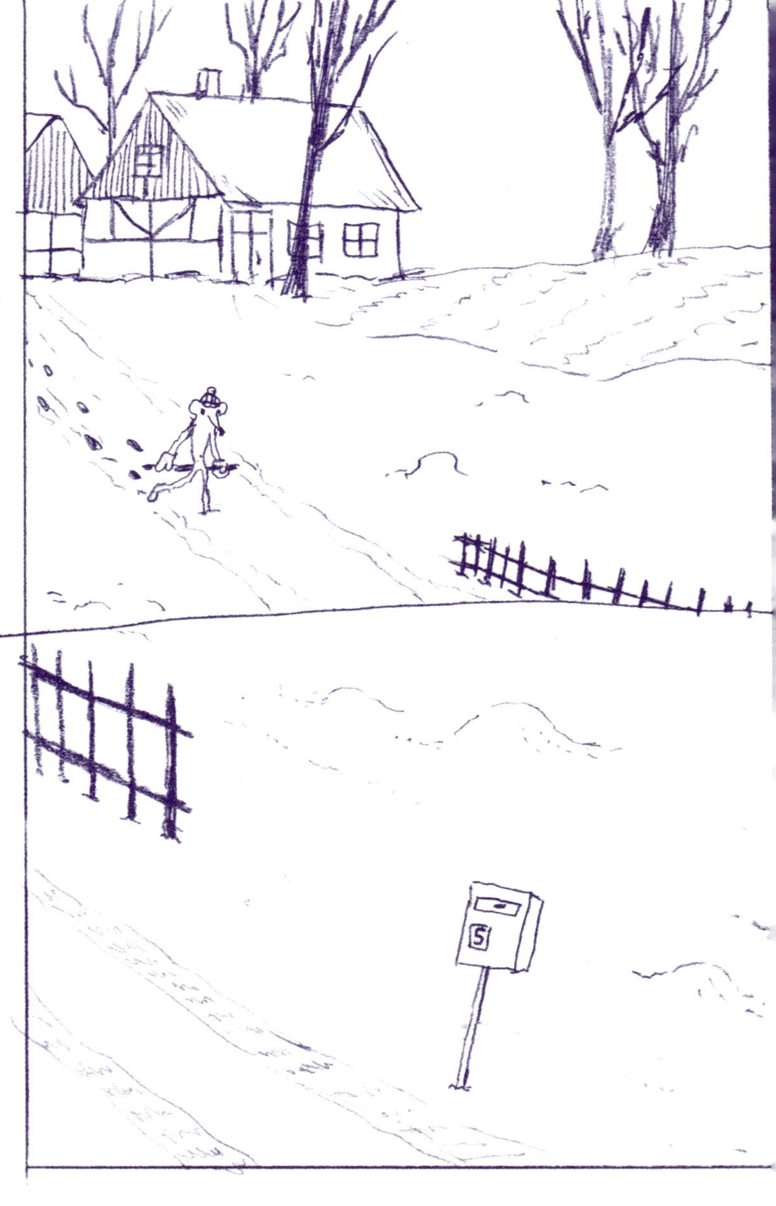

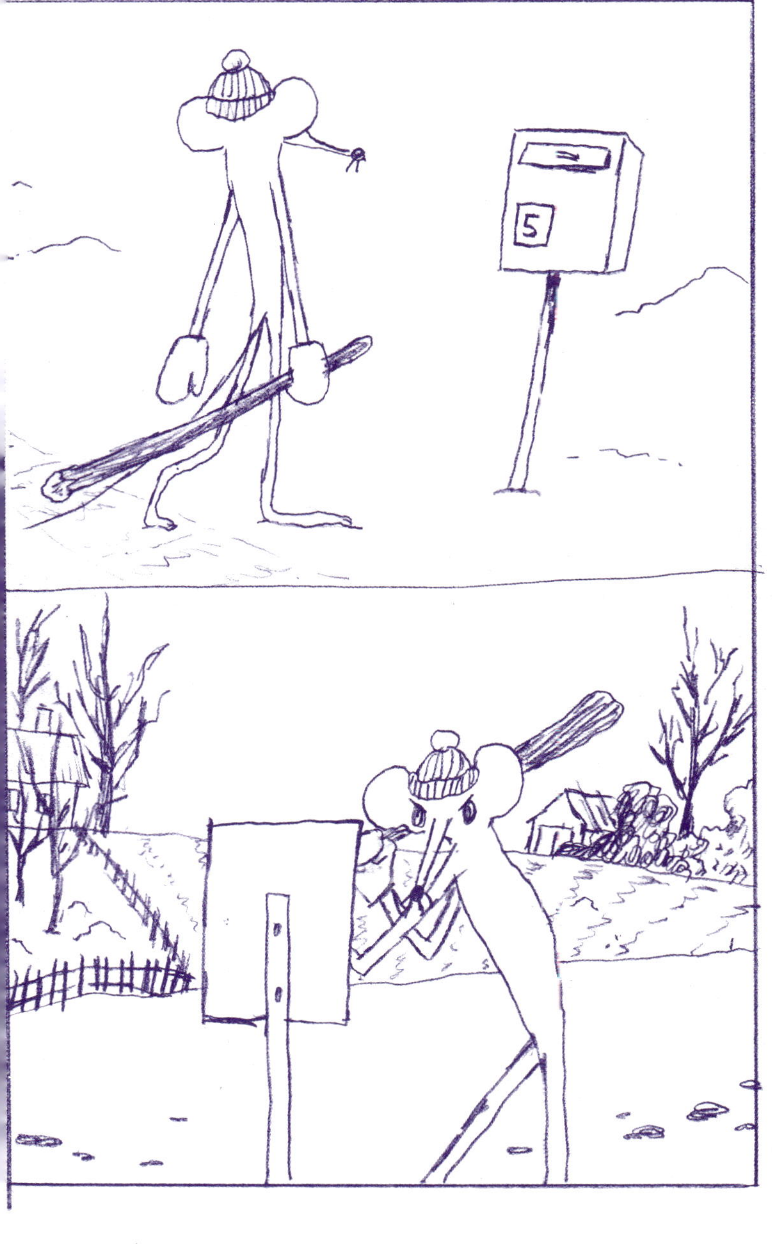

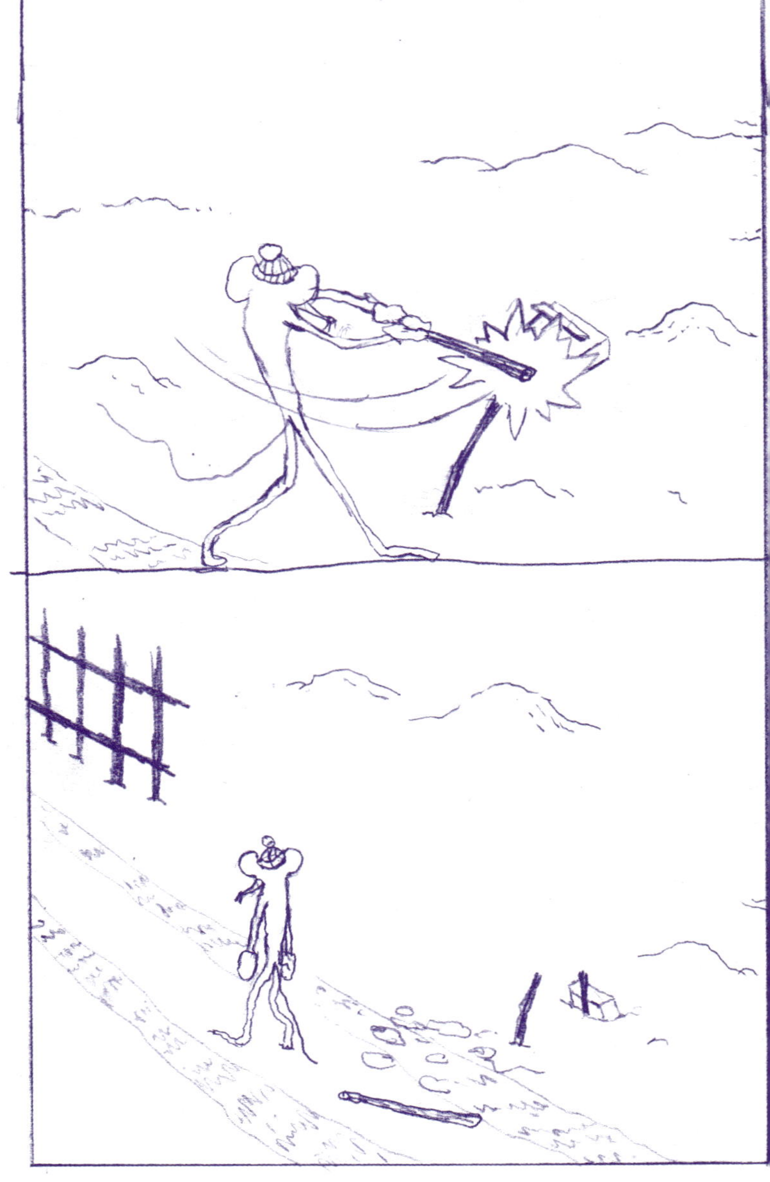

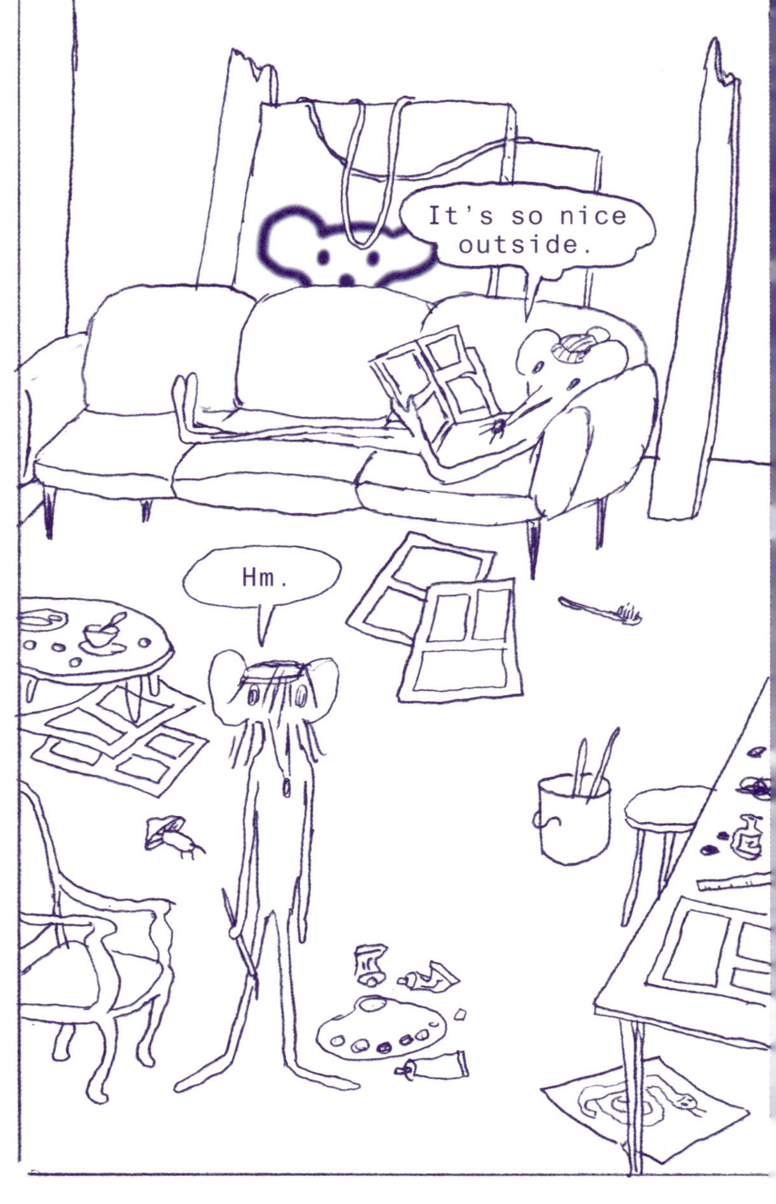
It's so nice outside.
Hm.

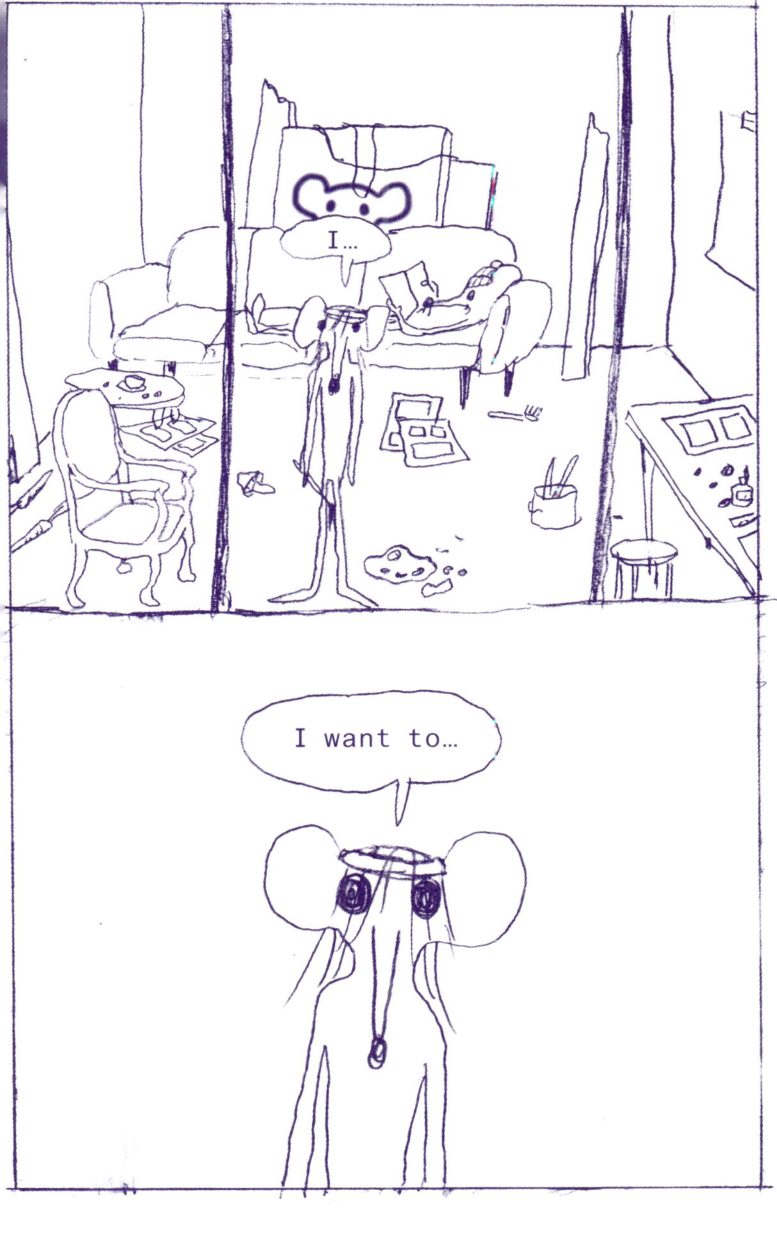

I...
I want to...

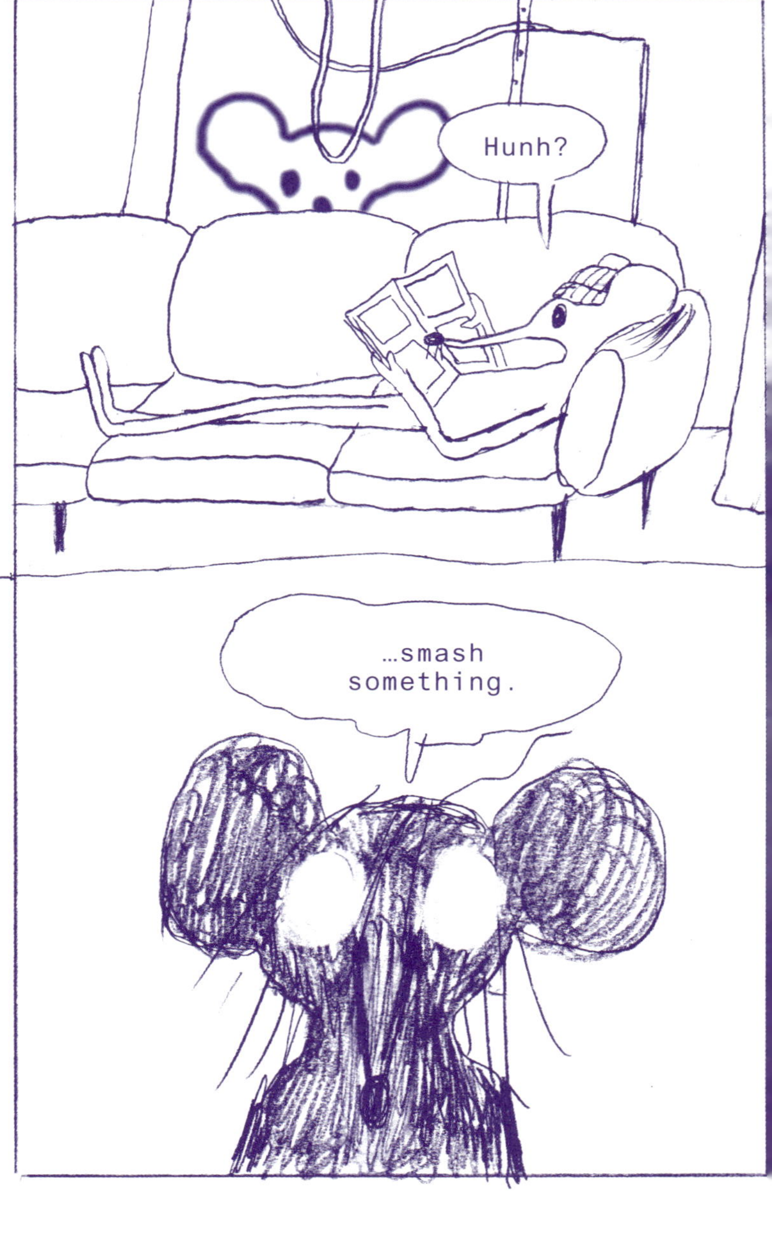
Hunh?
...smash
something.

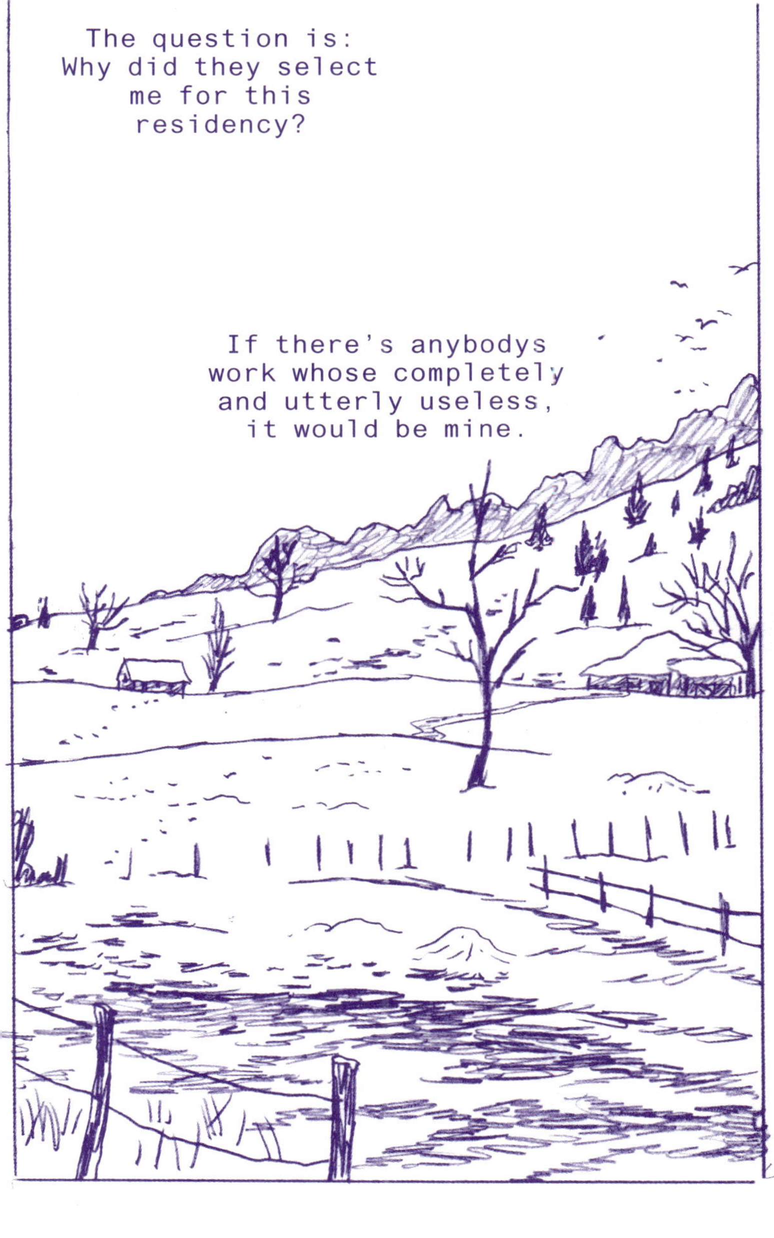

The question is:
Why did they select
me for this
residency?
If there's anybodys
work whose completely
and utterly useless,
it would be mine.

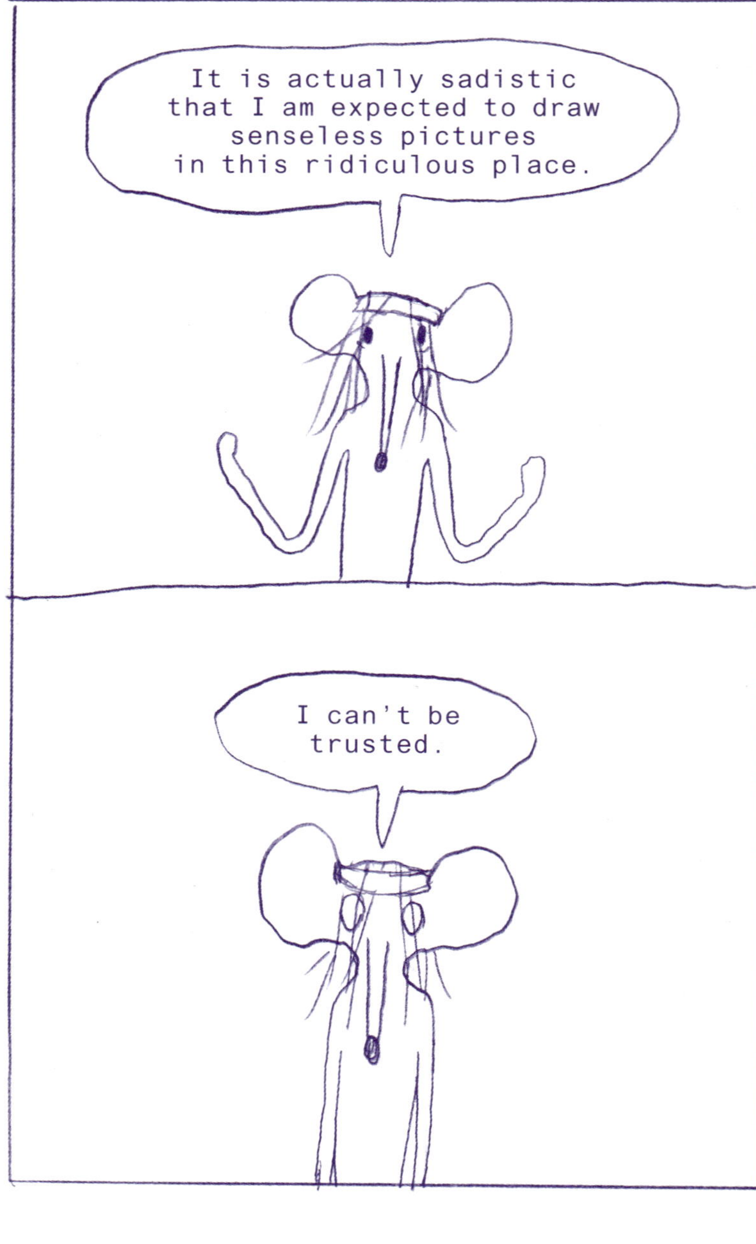

It is actually sadistic
that I am expected to draw
senseless pictures
in this ridiculous place.

I can't be
trusted.

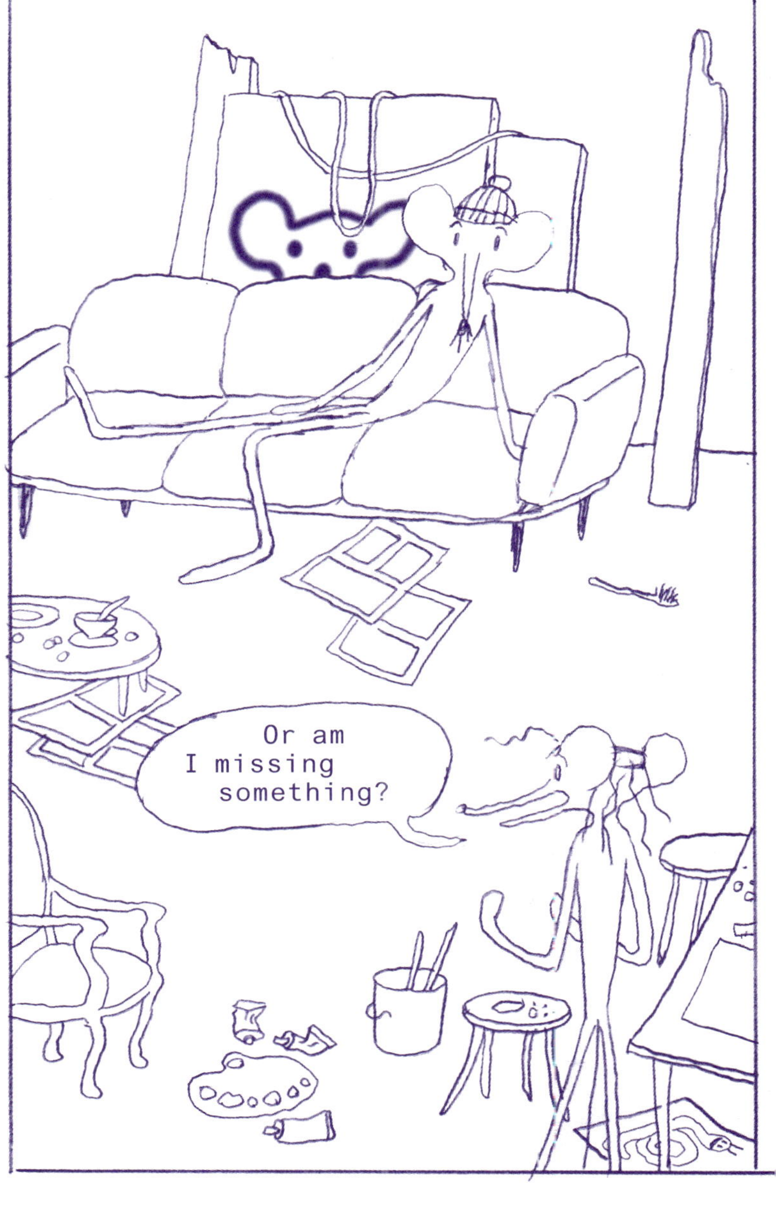

Or am
I missing
something?

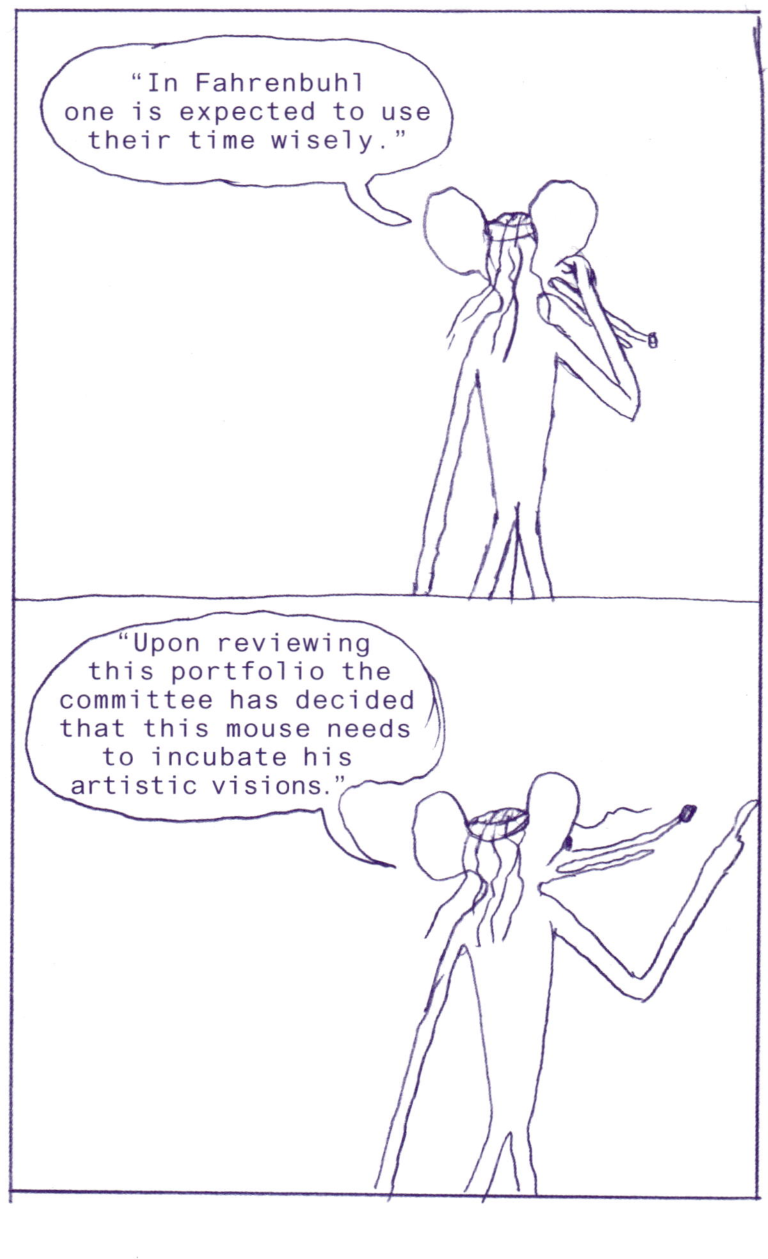

"In Fahrenbuhl
one is expected to use
their time wisely."

"Upon reviewing
this portfolio the
committee has decided
that this mouse needs
to incubate his
artistic visions."

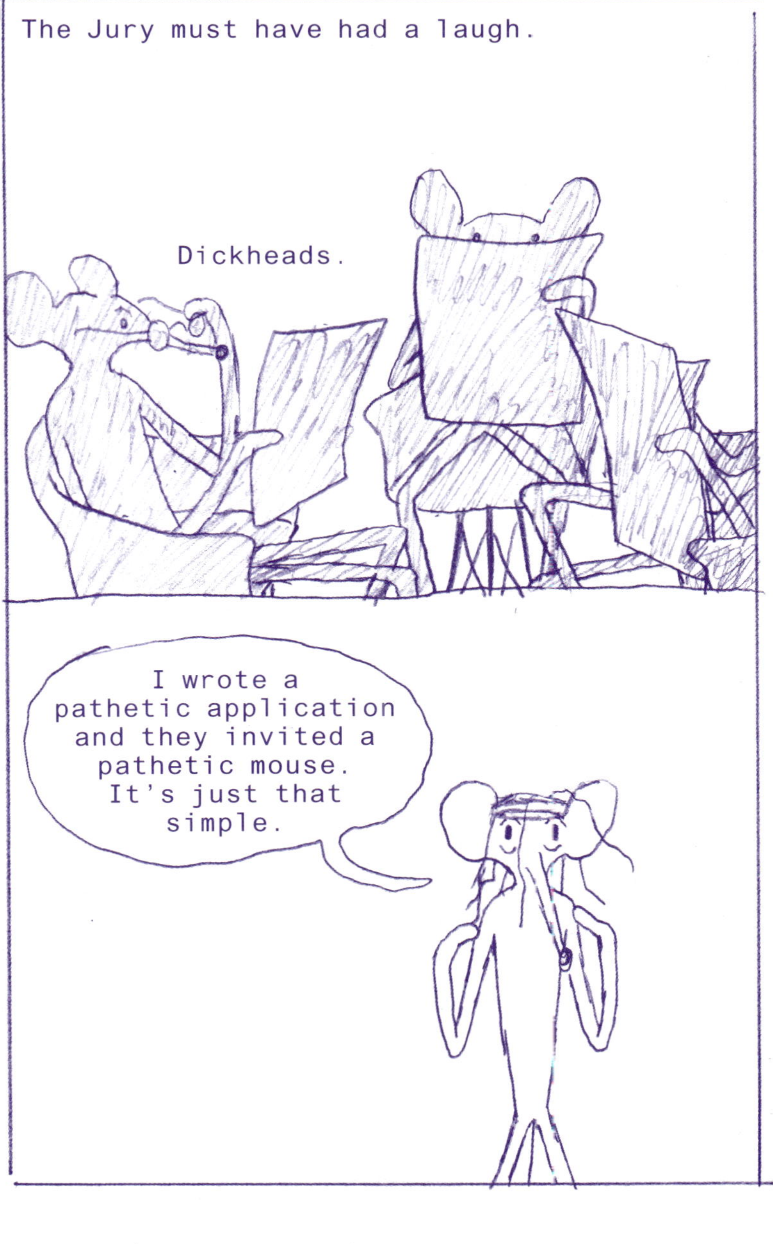

The Jury must have had a laugh.
Dickheads.
I wrote a
pathetic application
and they invited a
pathetic mouse.
It's just that
simple.

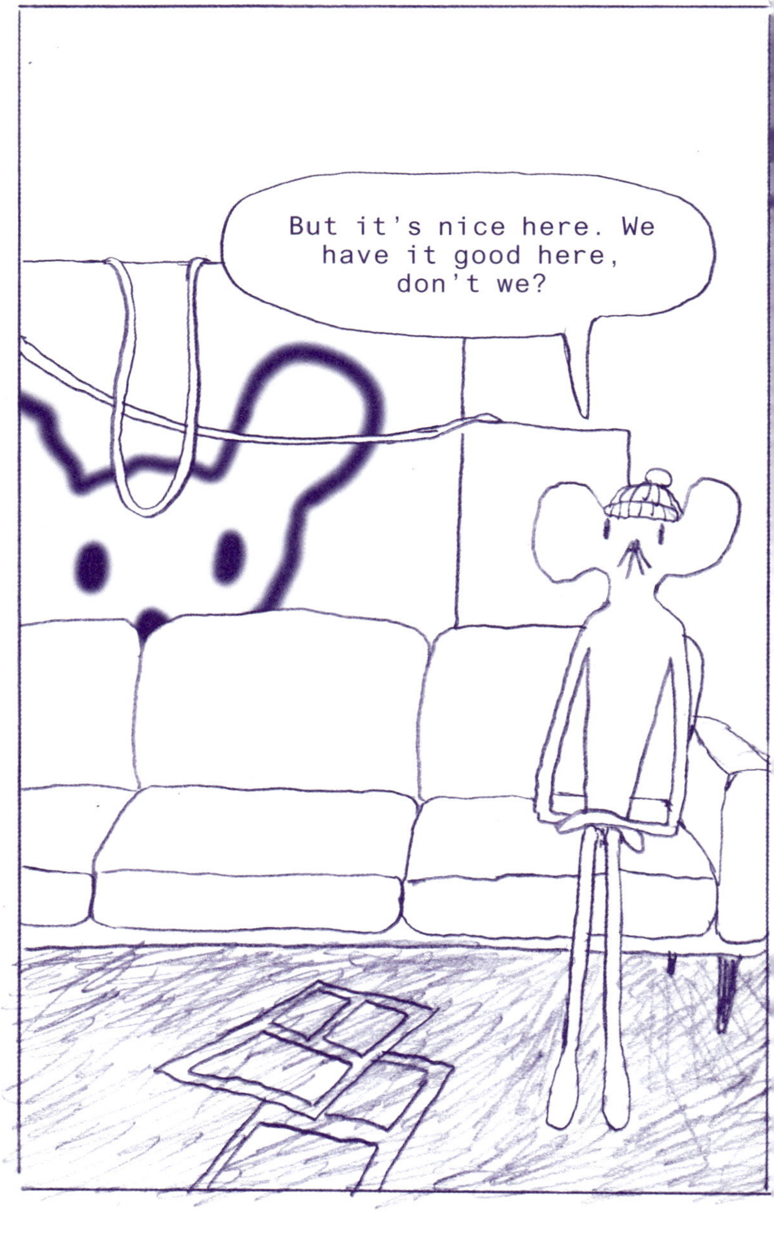
But it's nice here. We have it good here, don't we?

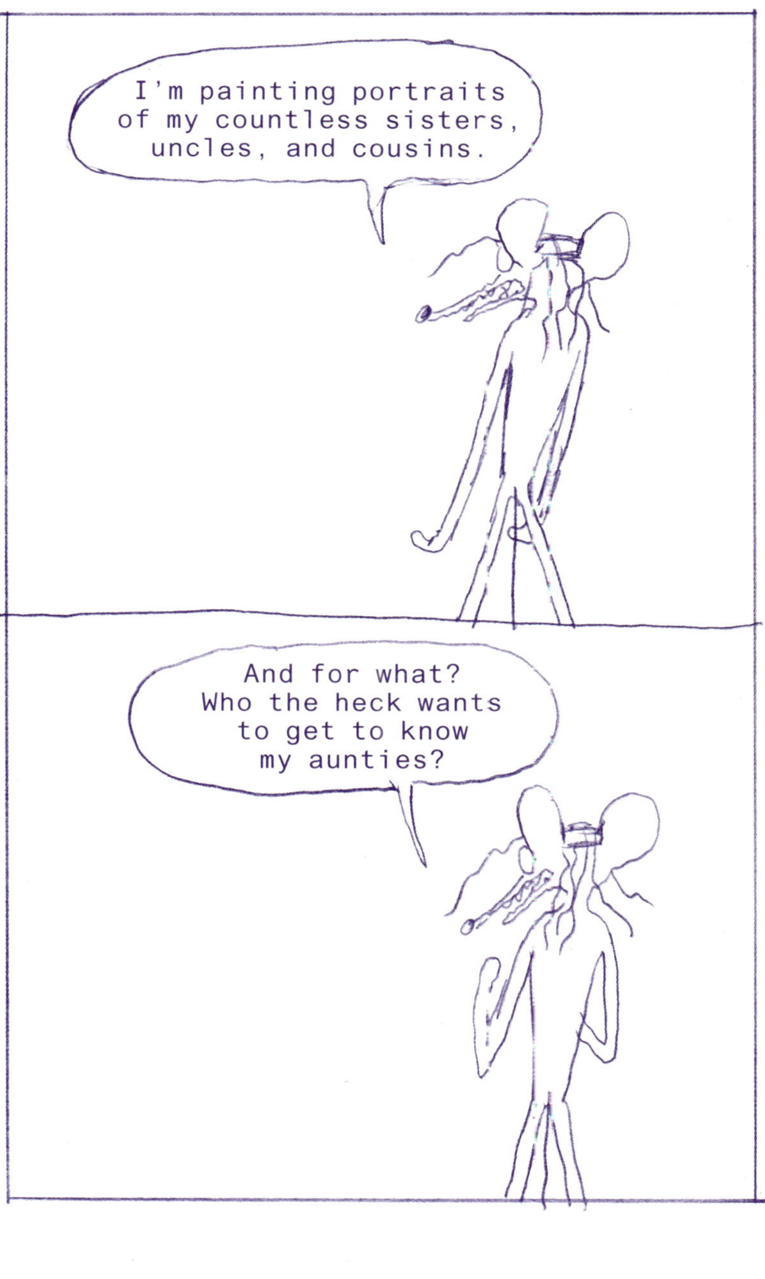

I'm painting portraits of my countless sisters, uncles, and cousins.
And for what? Who the heck wants to get to know my aunties?

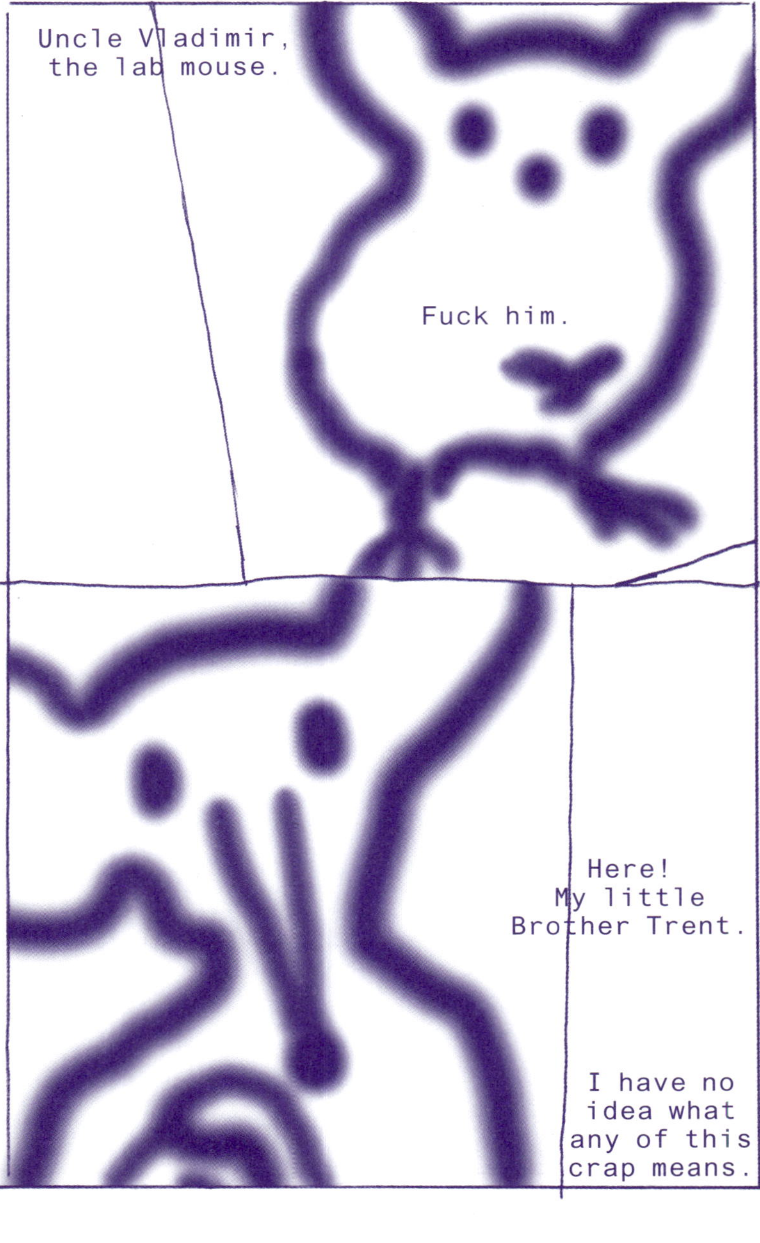
Uncle Vladimir,
the lab mouse.
Fuck him.
Here!
My little
Brother Trent.
I have no
idea what
any of this
crap means.

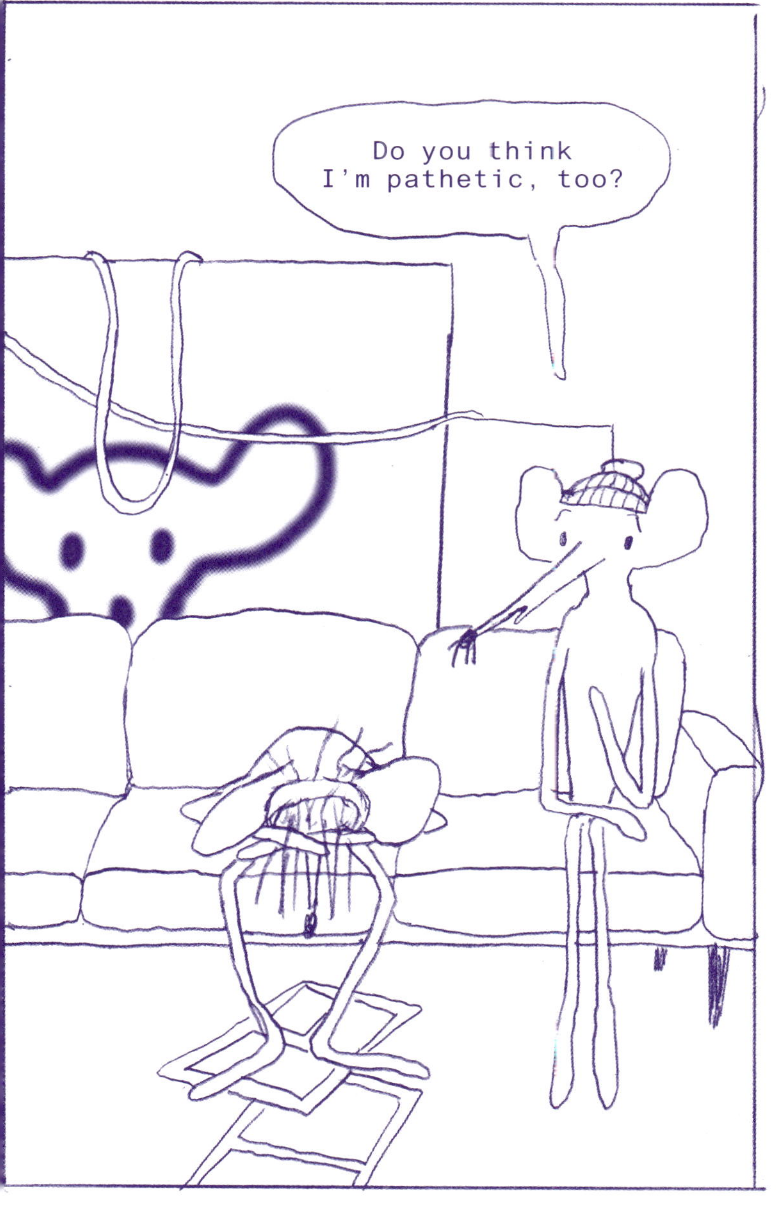

Do you think
I'm pathetic, too?

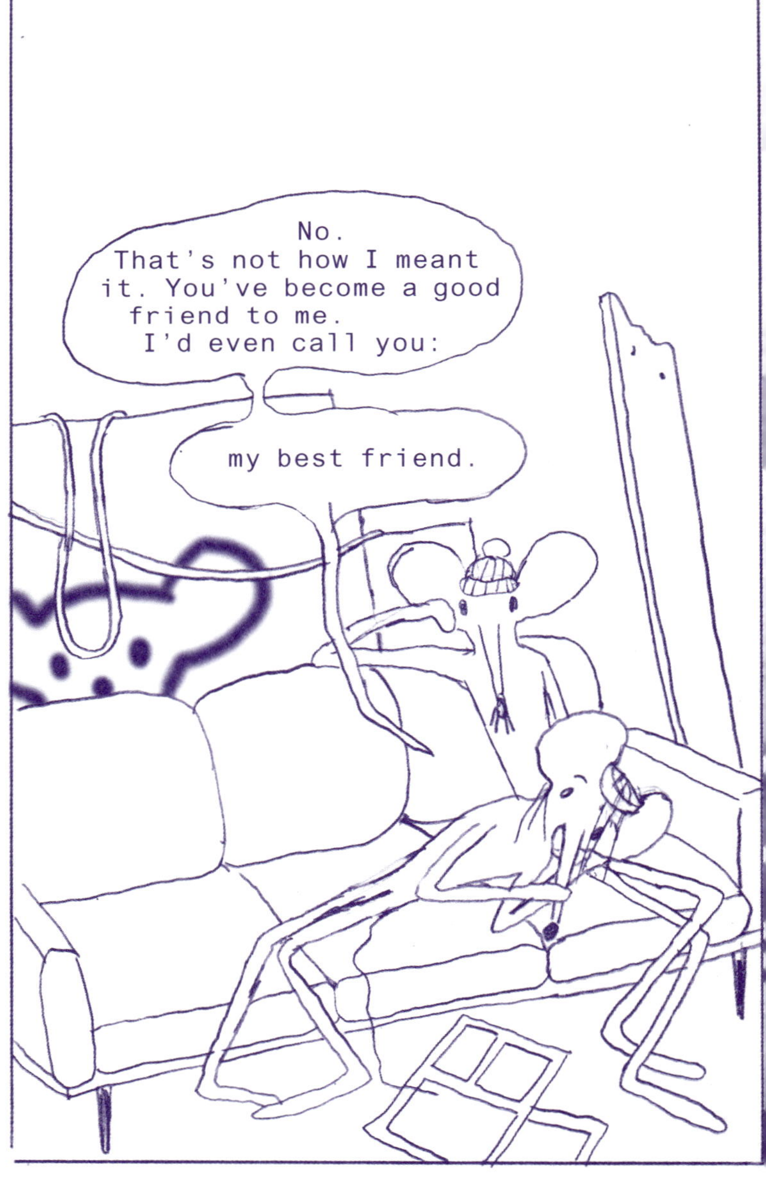

No.
That's not how I meant it. You've become a good friend to me.
I'd even call you:
my best friend.

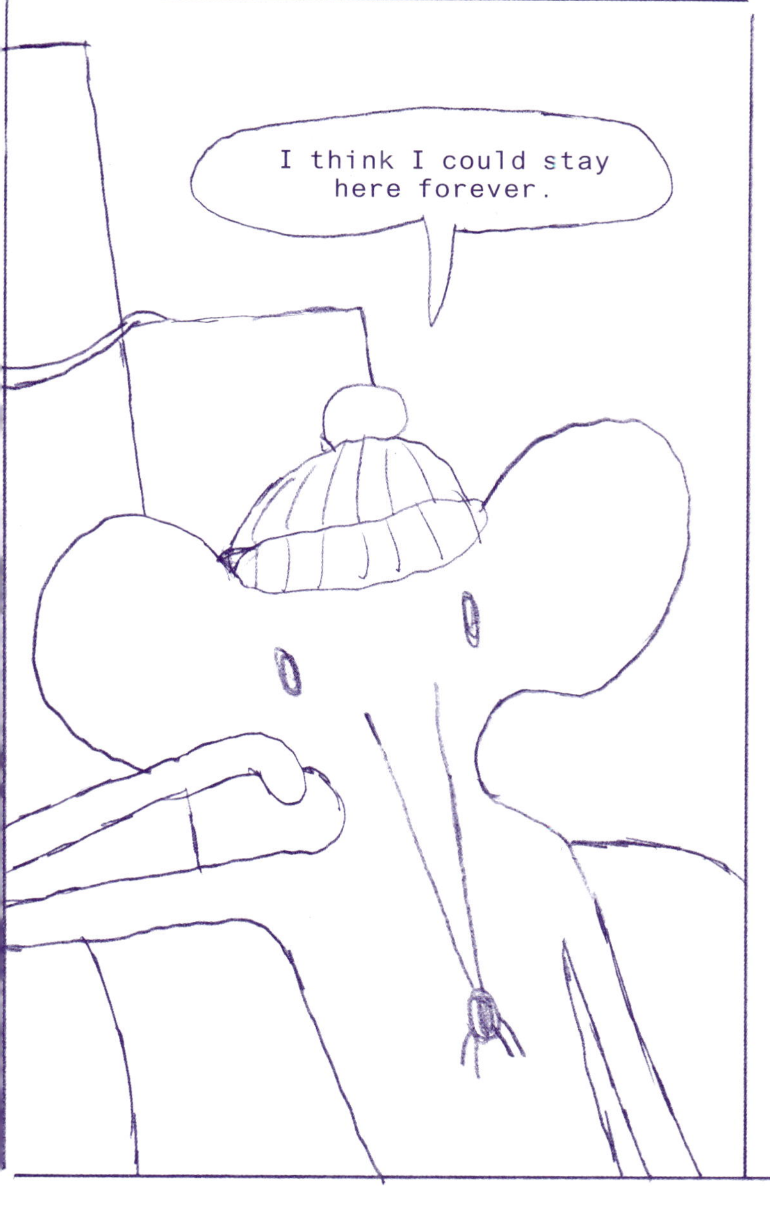

I think I could stay
here forever.

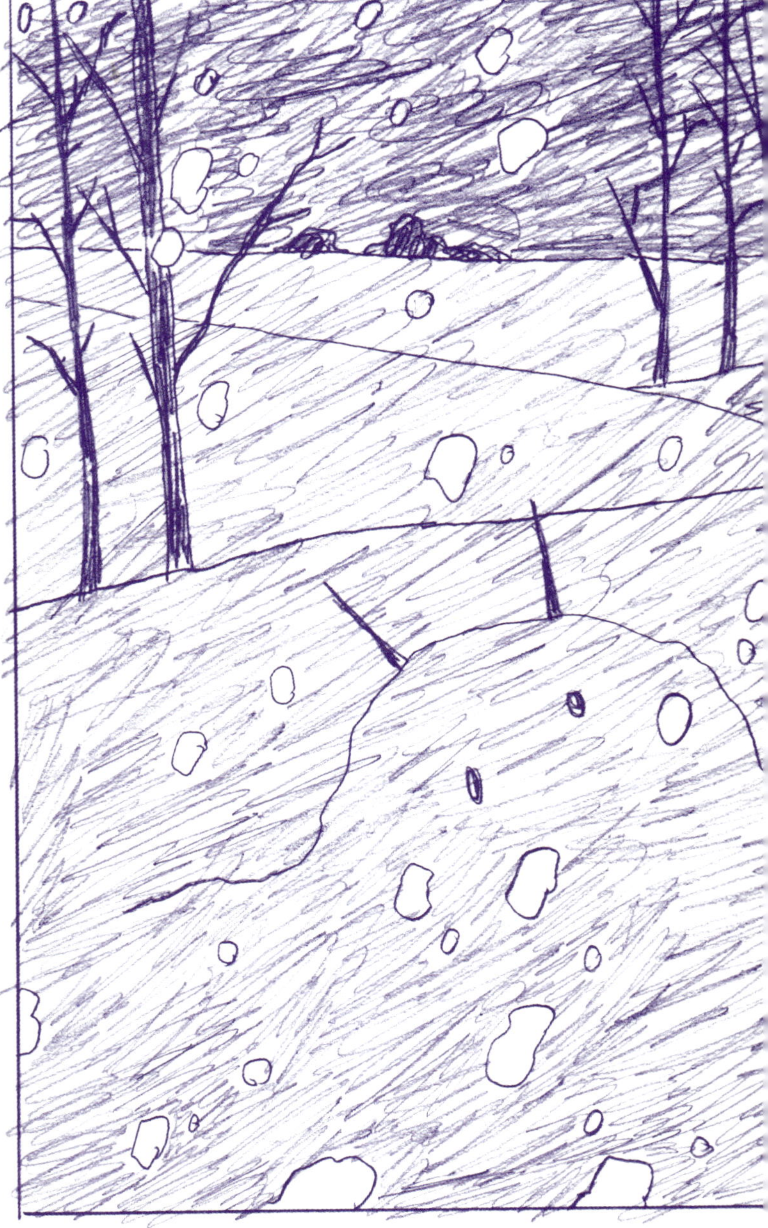

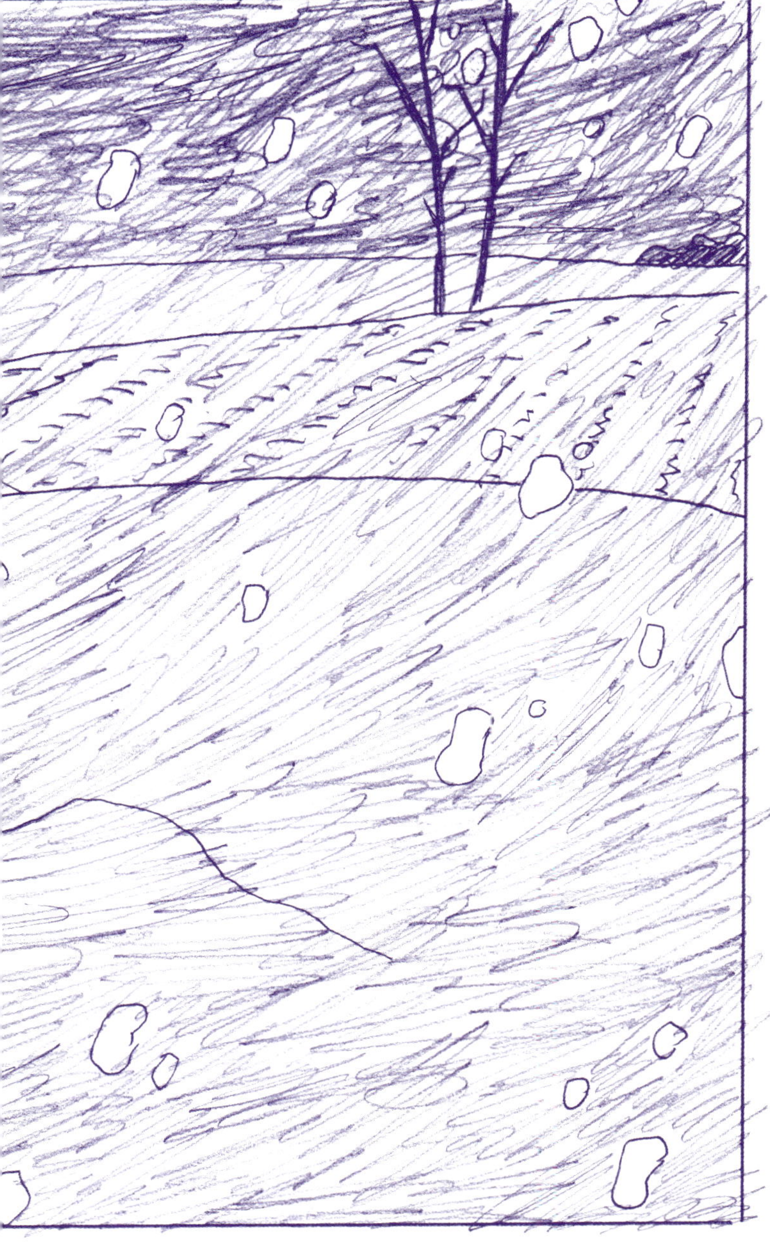

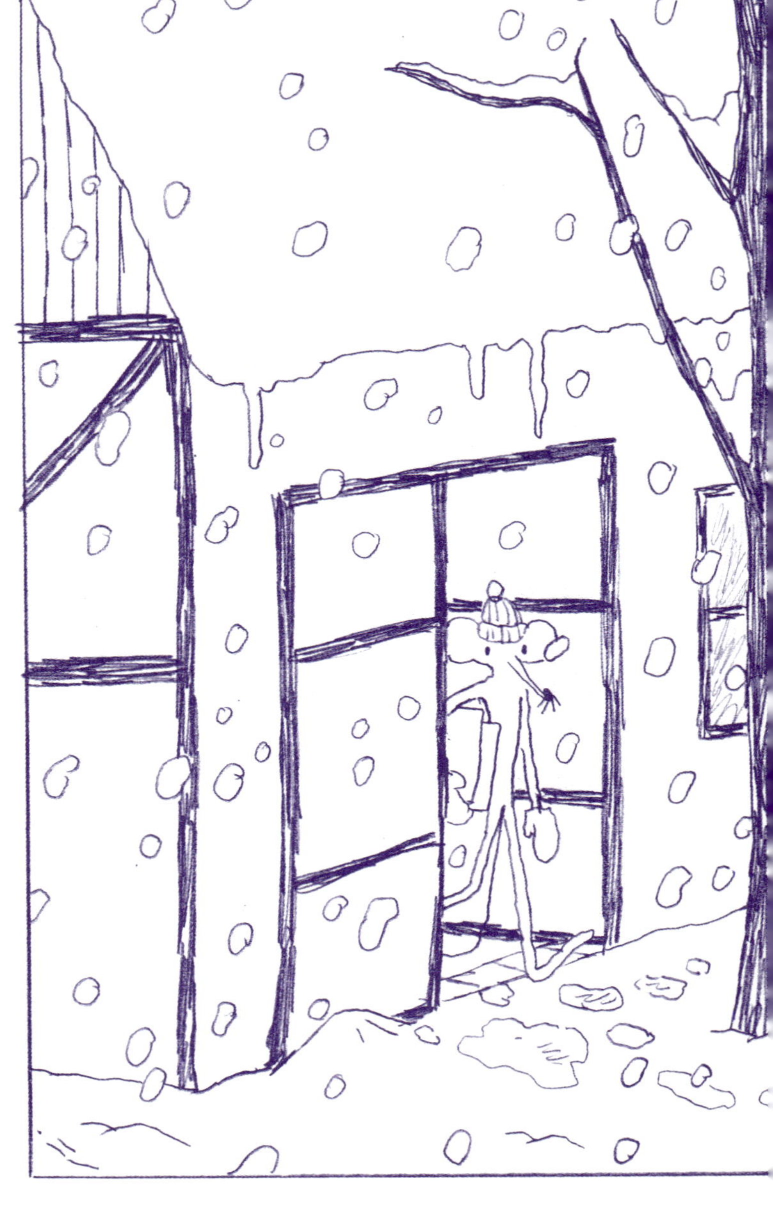

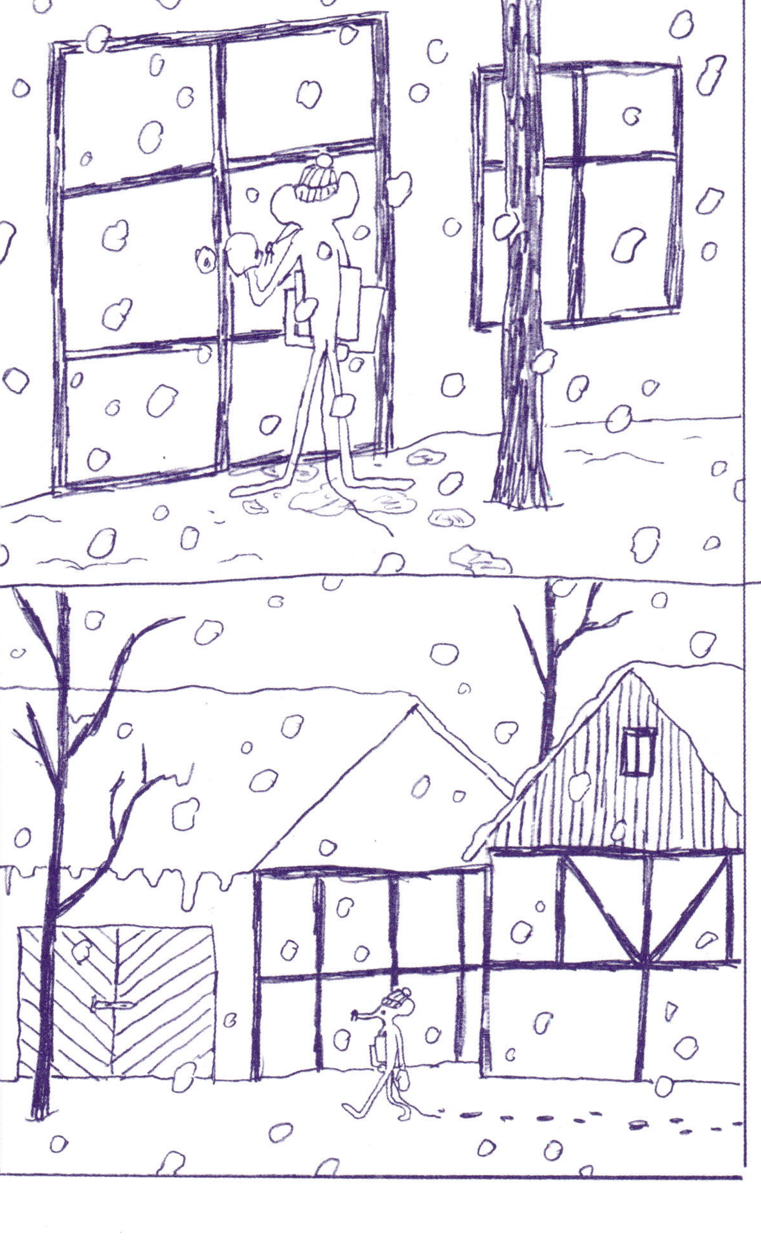

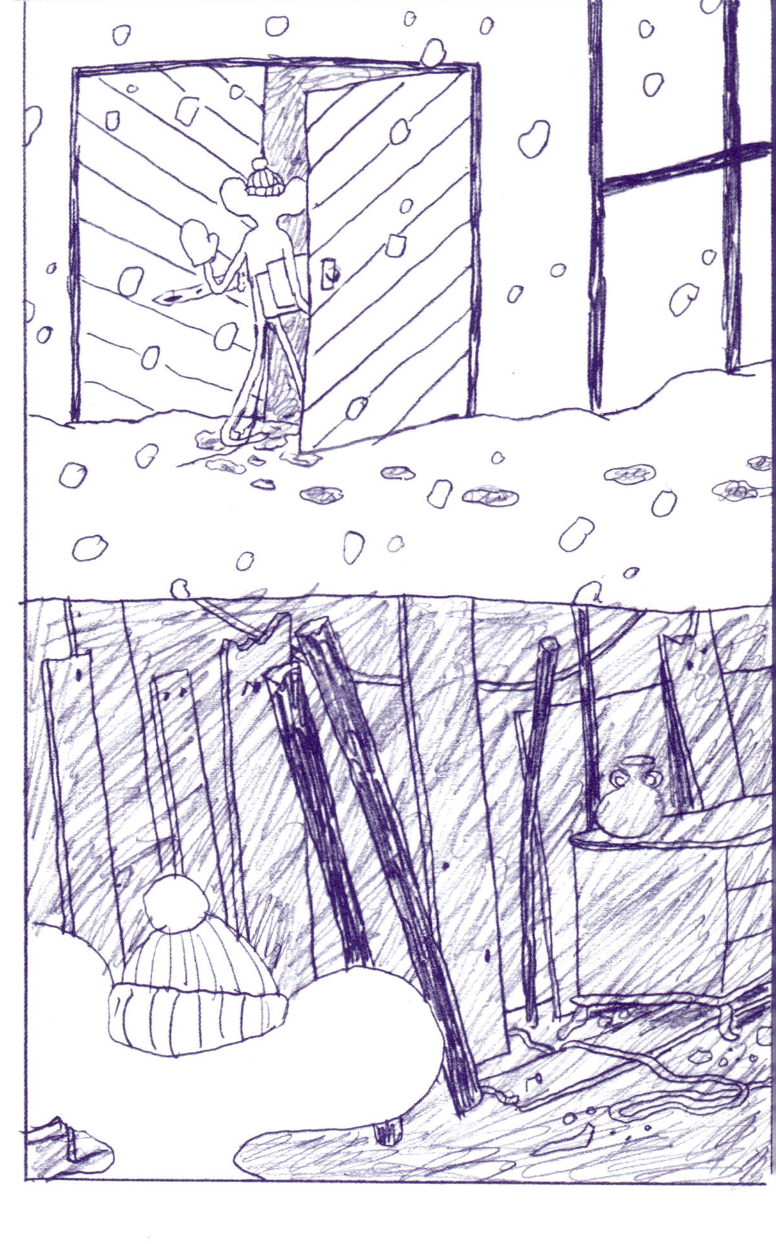

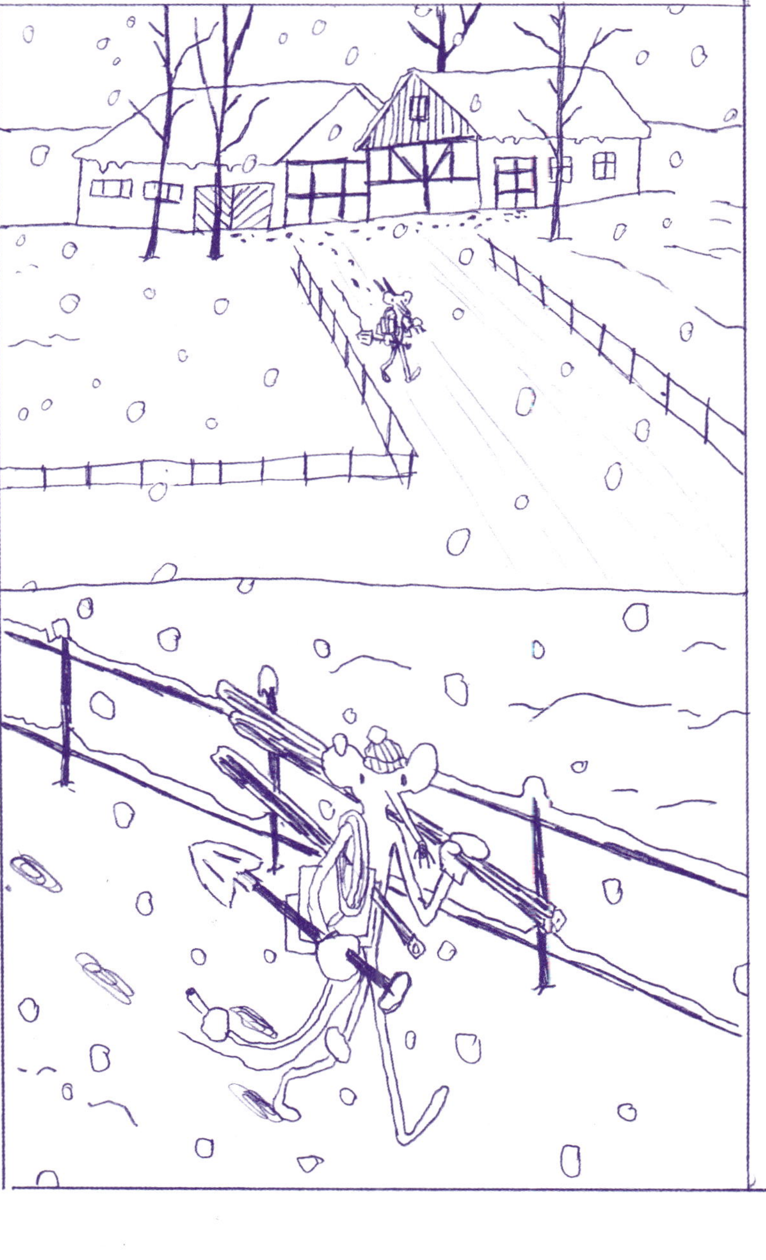

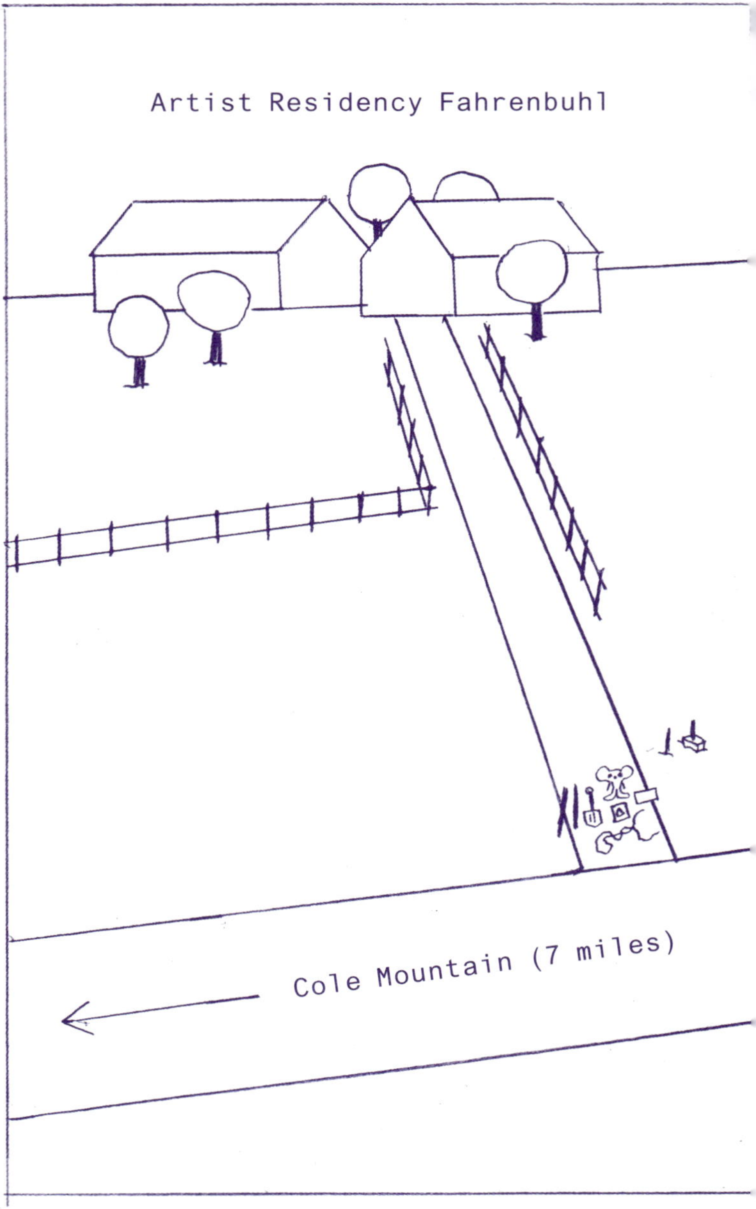

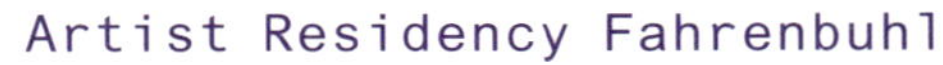

Artist Residency Fahrenbuhl
Cole Mountain (7 miles)

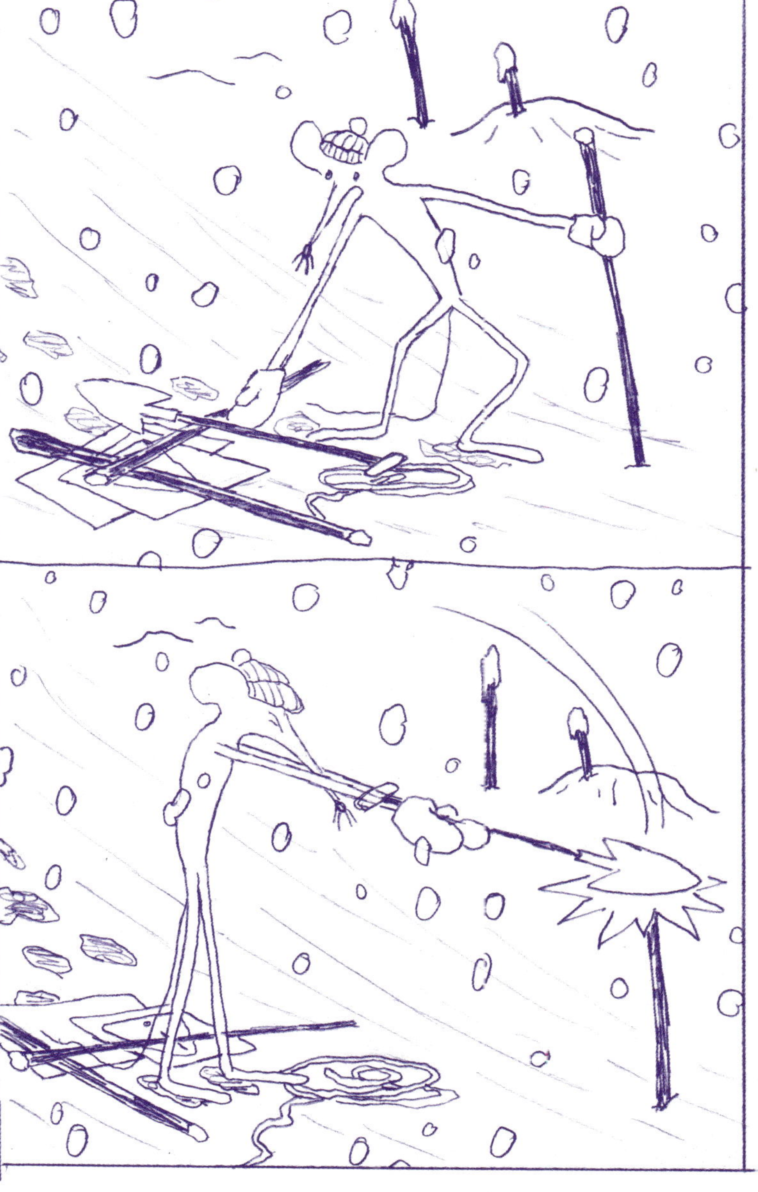

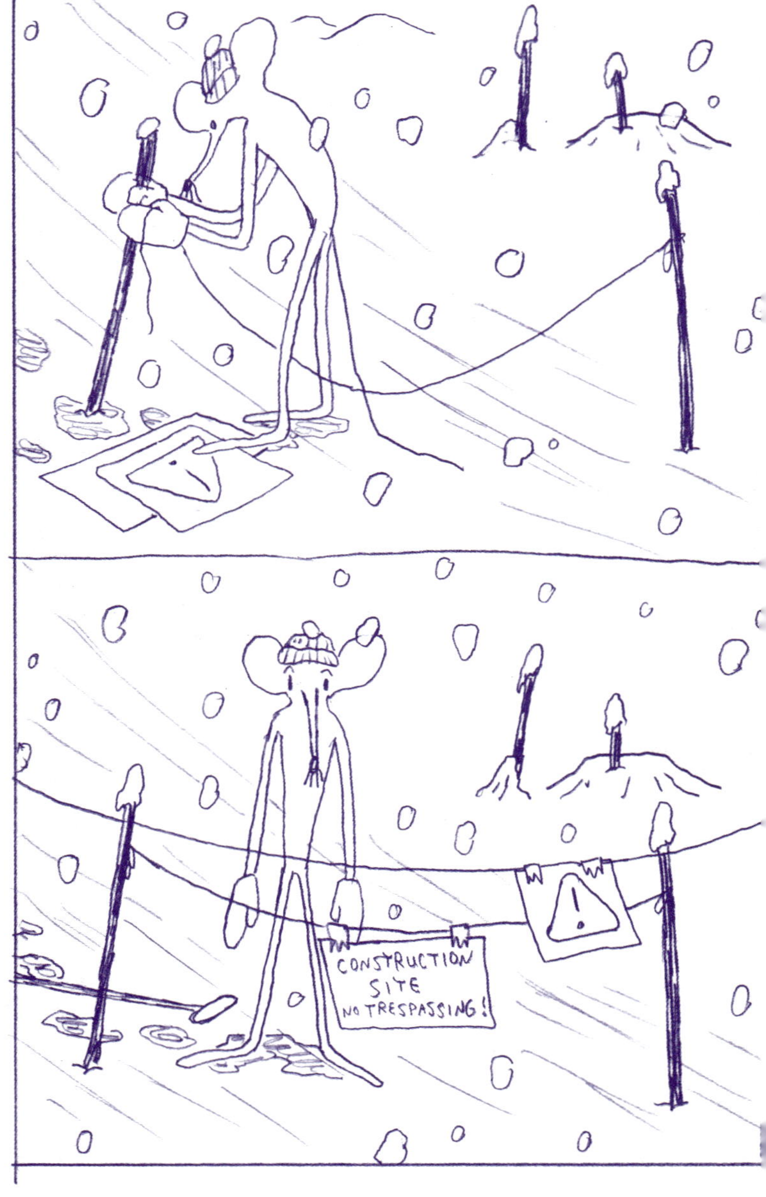

CONSTRUCTION
SITE
NO TRESPASSING!

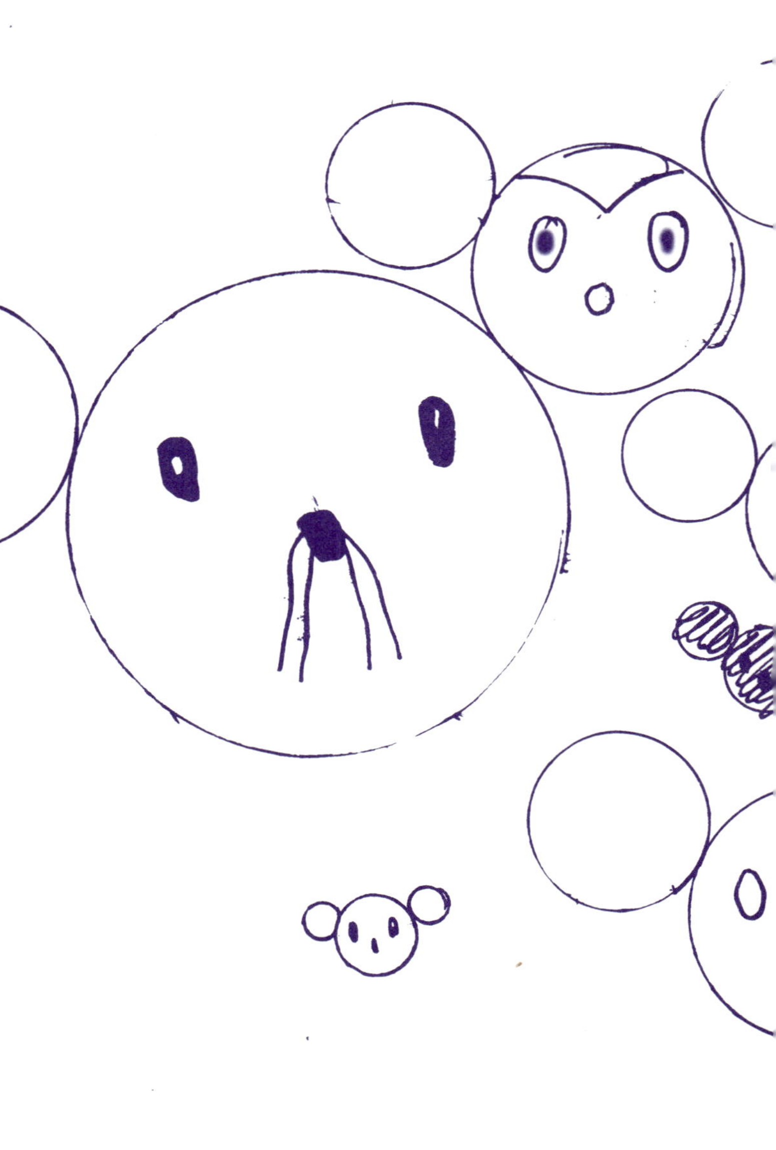

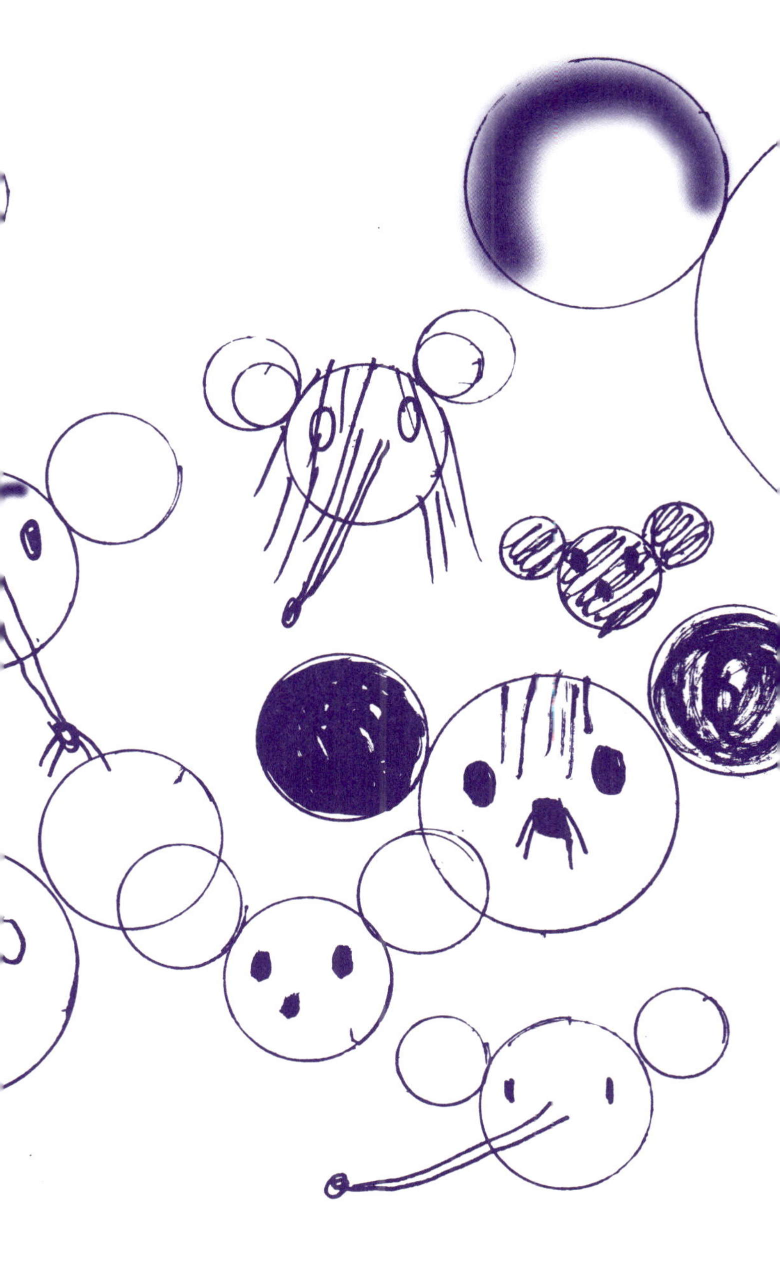

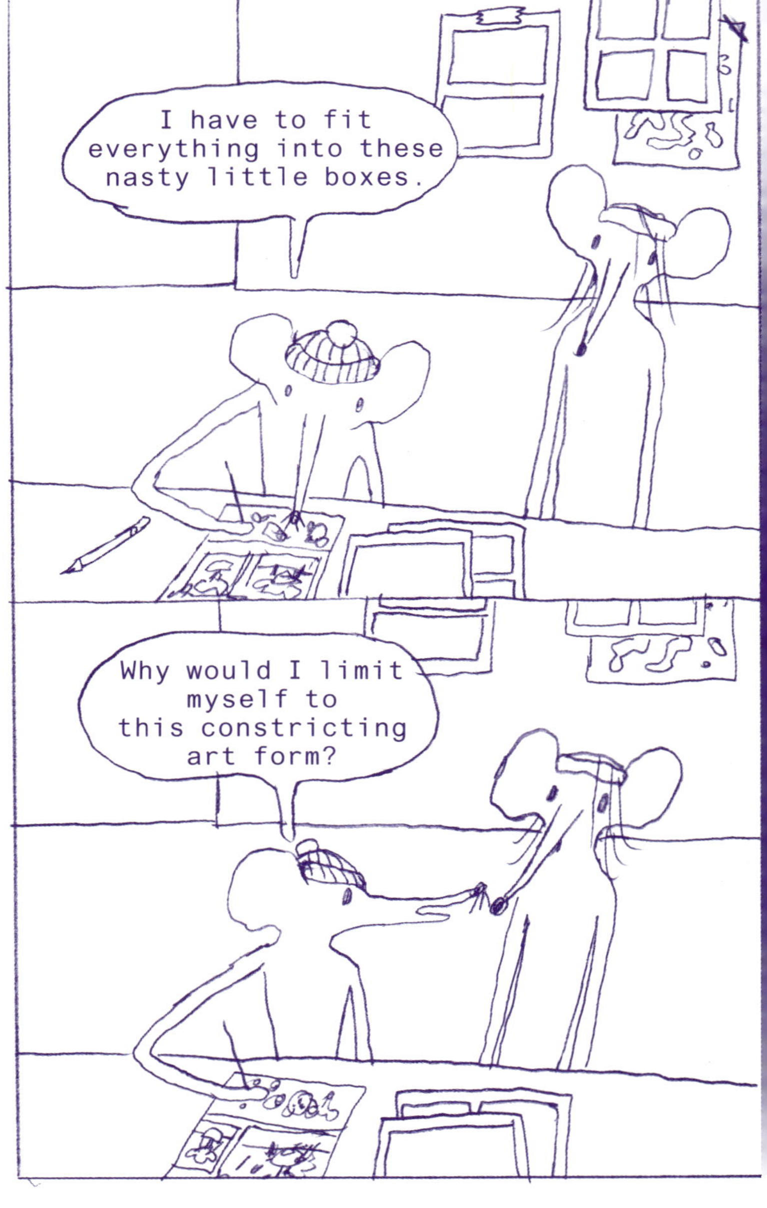

I have to fit everything into these nasty little boxes.
Why would I limit myself to this constricting art form?

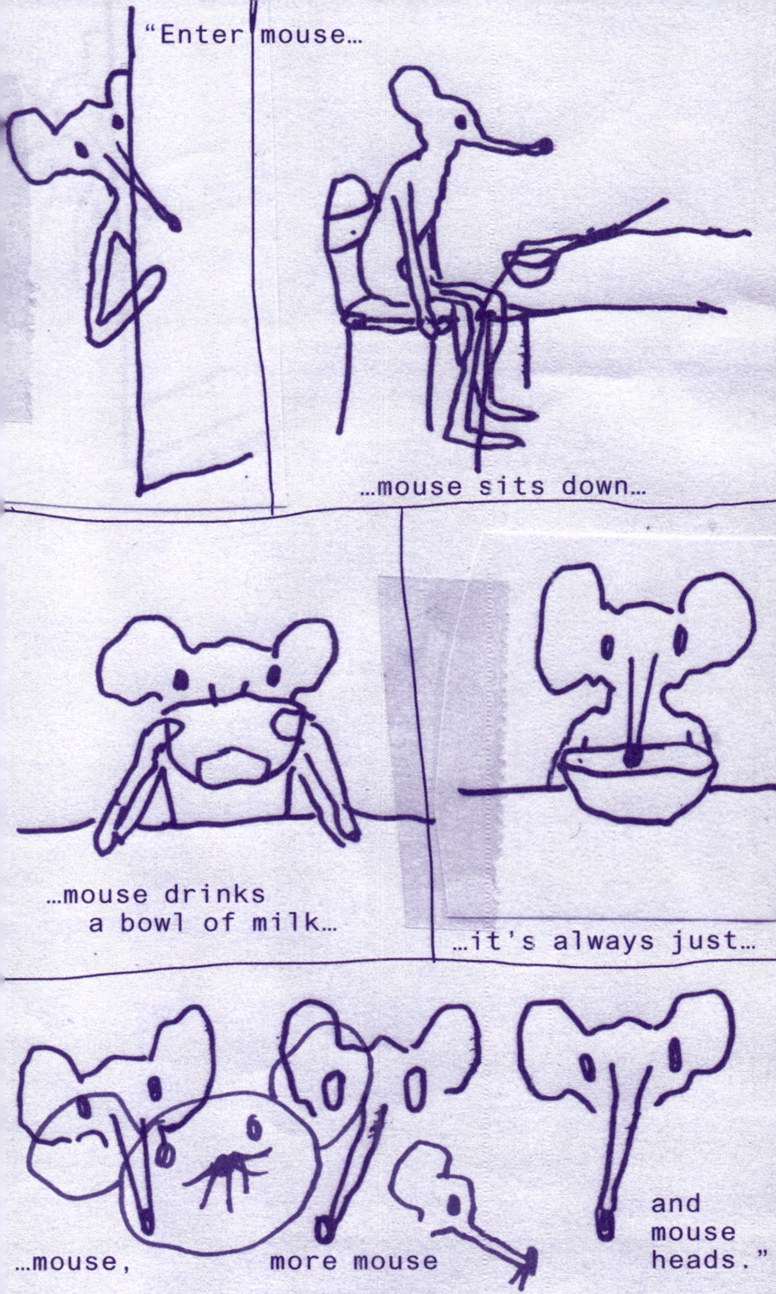

"Enter mouse...
...mouse sits down...
...mouse drinks
a bowl of milk...
...it's always just...
...mouse,
more mouse
and
mouse
heads."

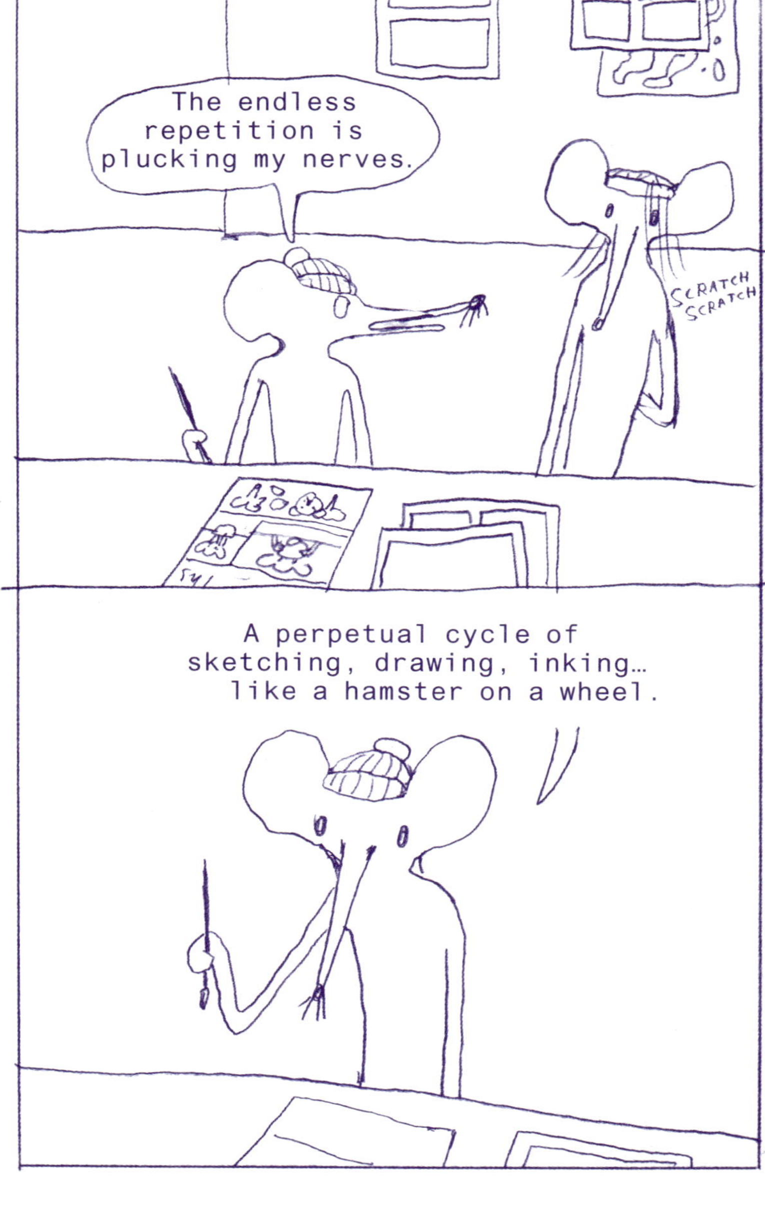
The endless repetition is plucking my nerves.
SCRATCH SCRATCH
A perpetual cycle of sketching, drawing, inking...
like a hamster on a wheel.

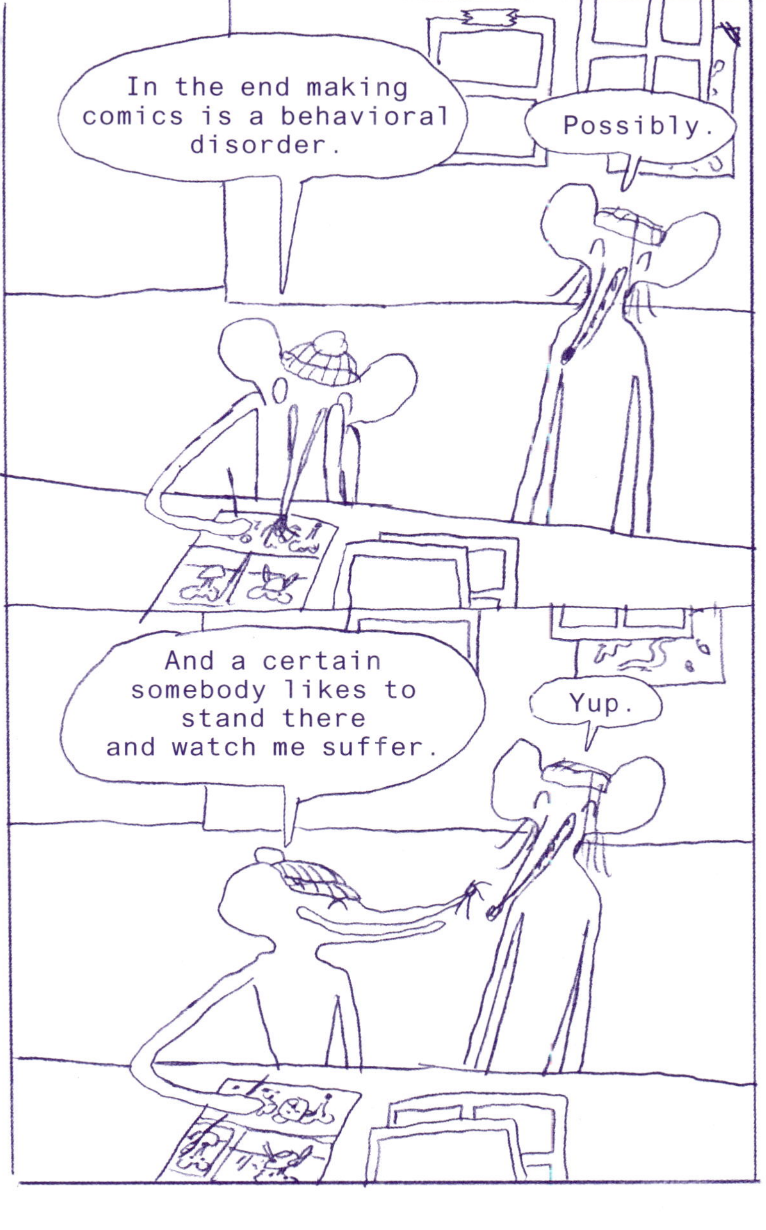

In the end making comics is a behavioral disorder.
Possibly.
And a certain somebody likes to stand there and watch me suffer.
Yup.

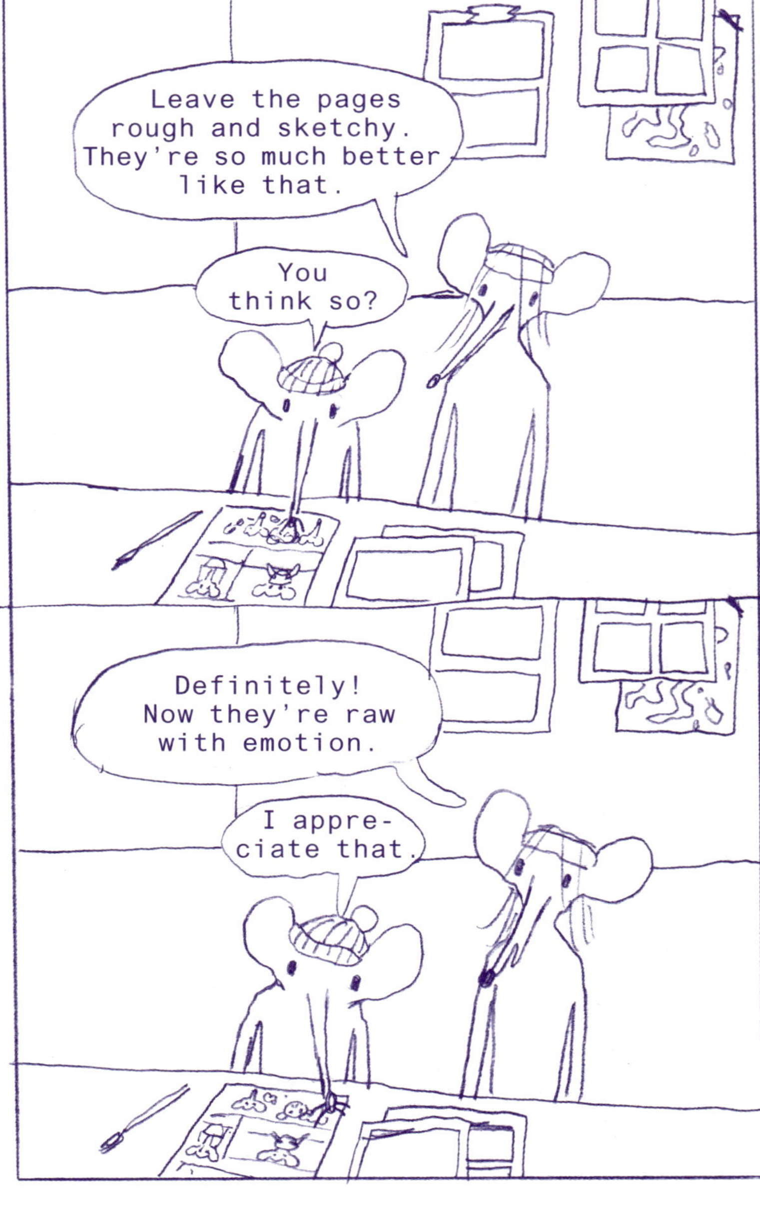

Leave the pages rough and sketchy. They're so much better like that.
You think so?
Definitely! Now they're raw with emotion.
I appreciate that.

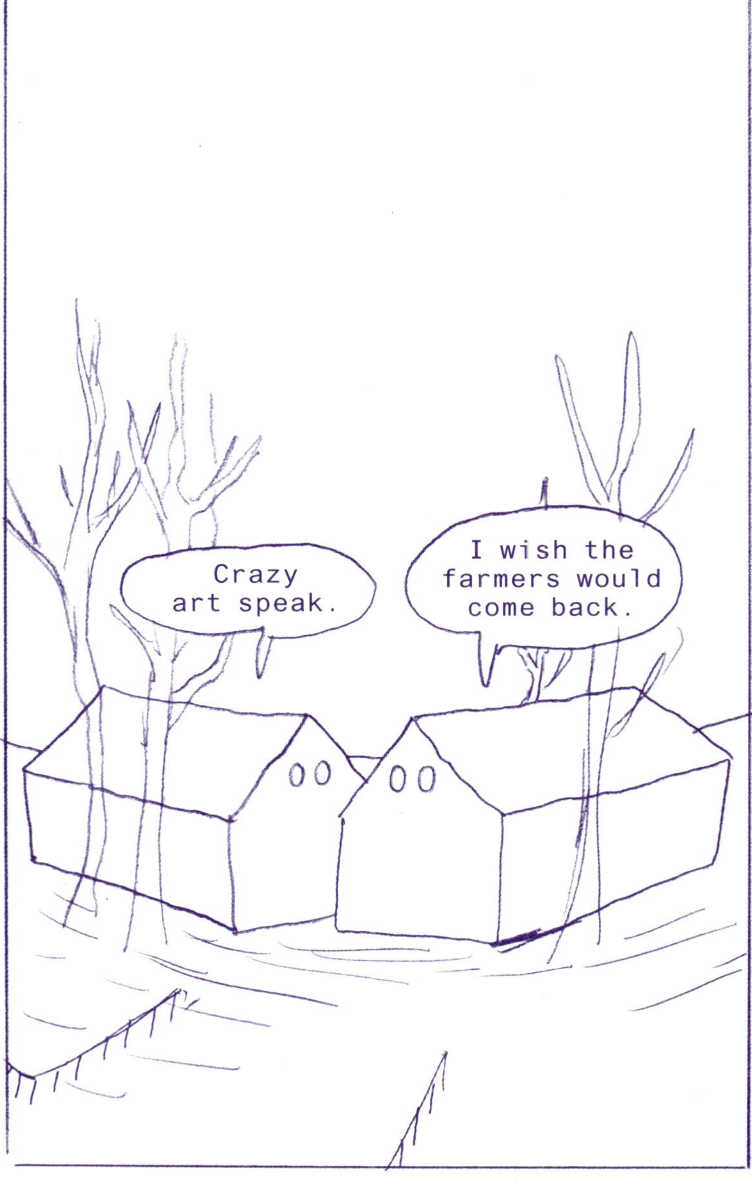

Crazy
art speak.

I wish the
farmers would
come back.

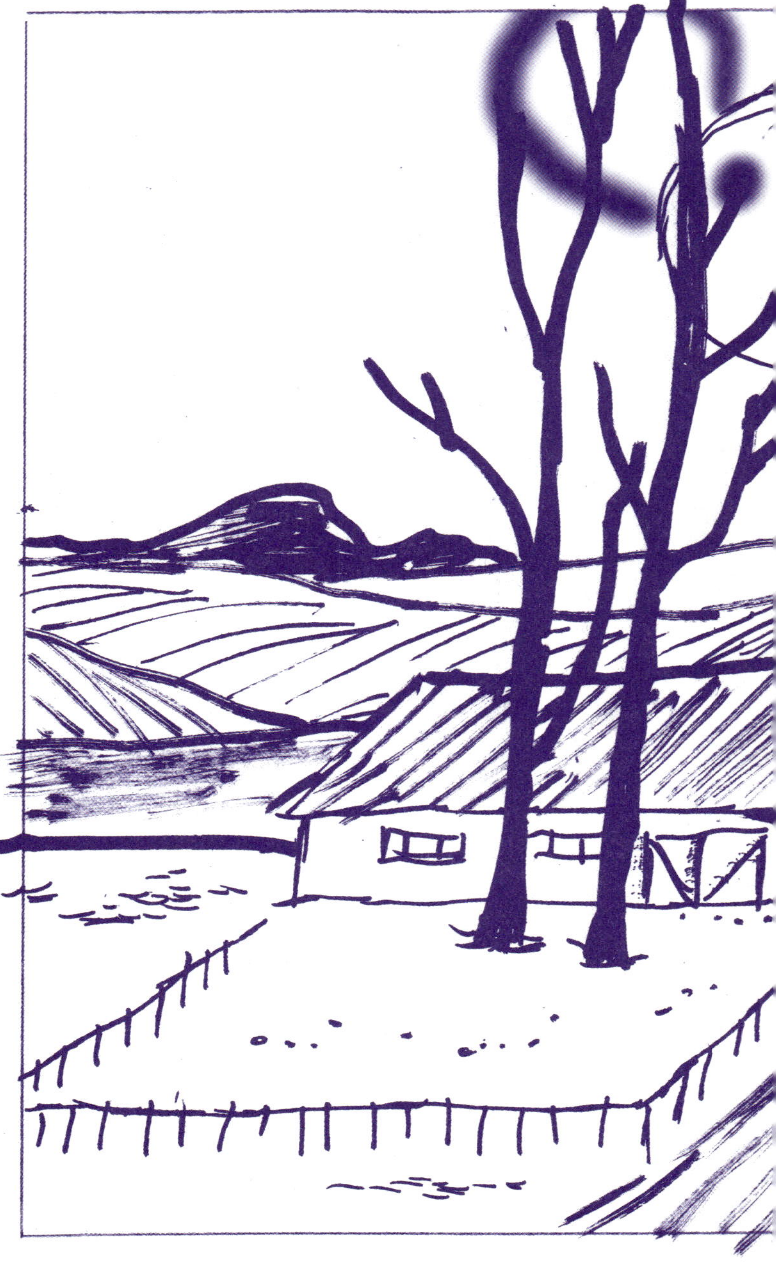

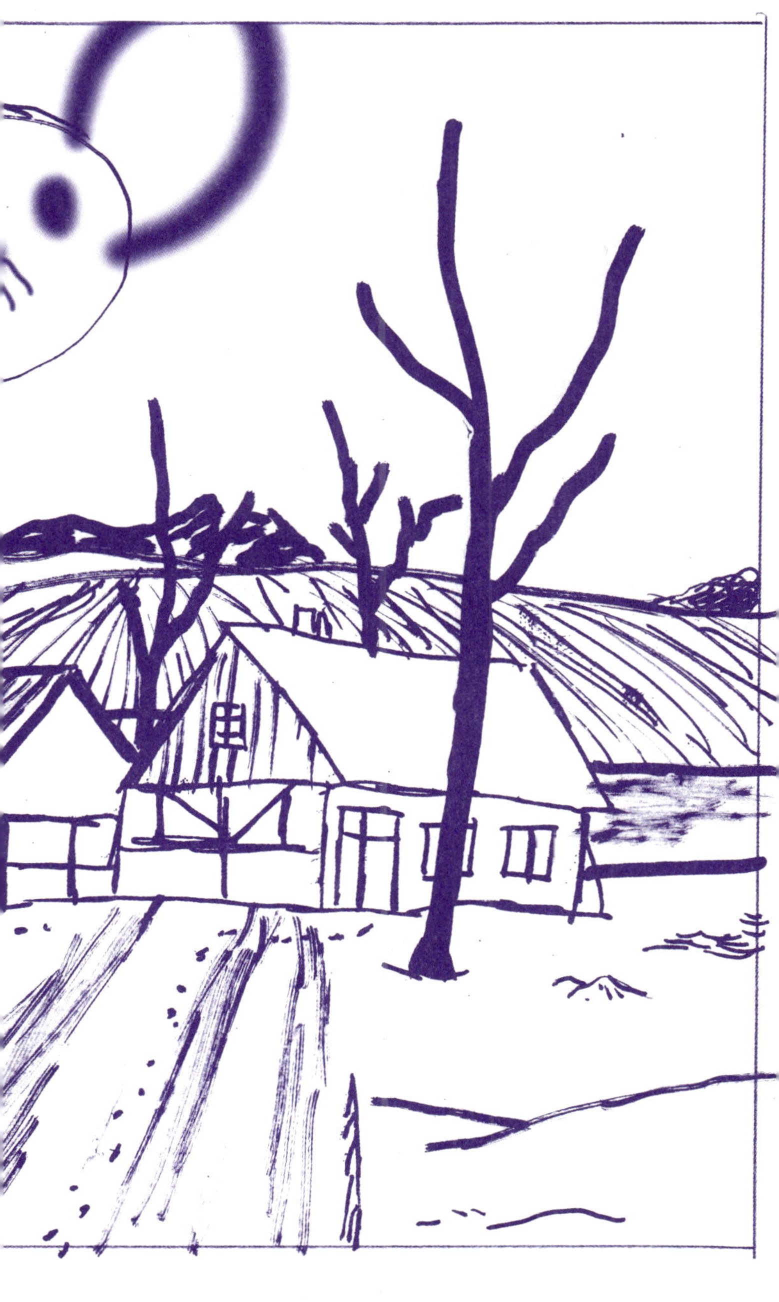

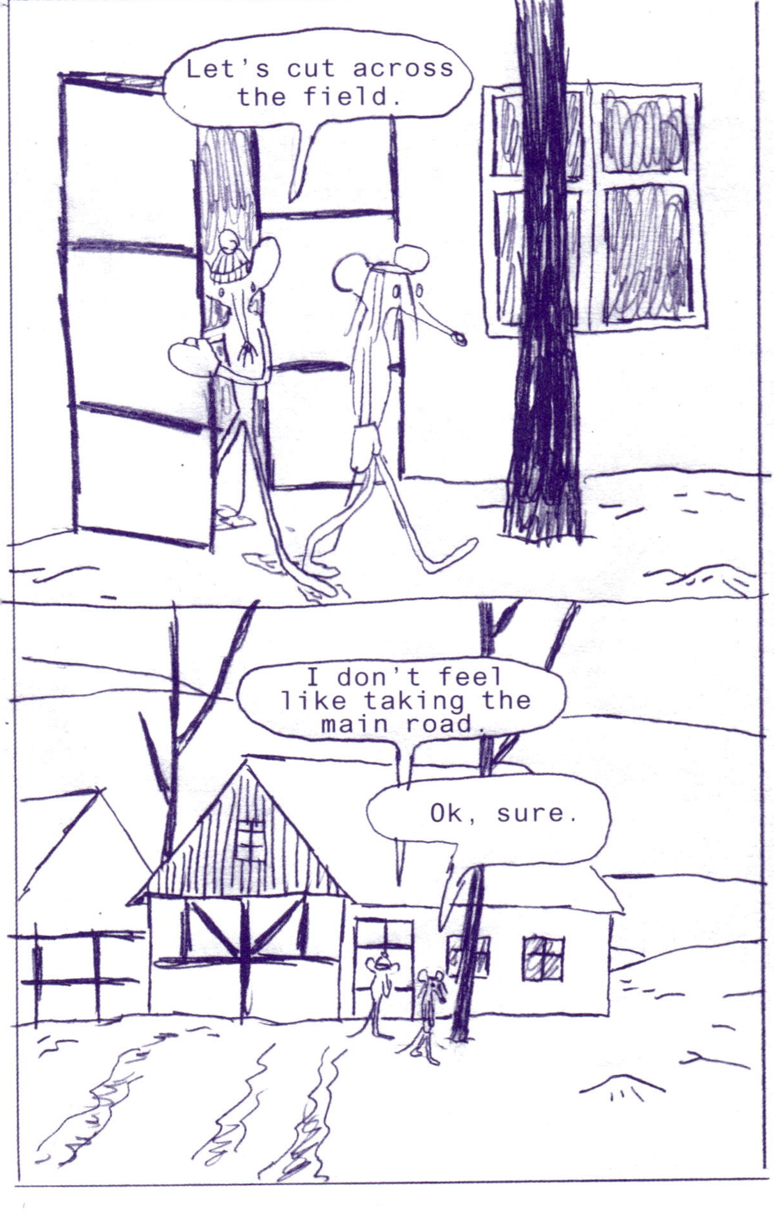

Let's cut across the field.
I don't feel like taking the main road.
Ok, sure.

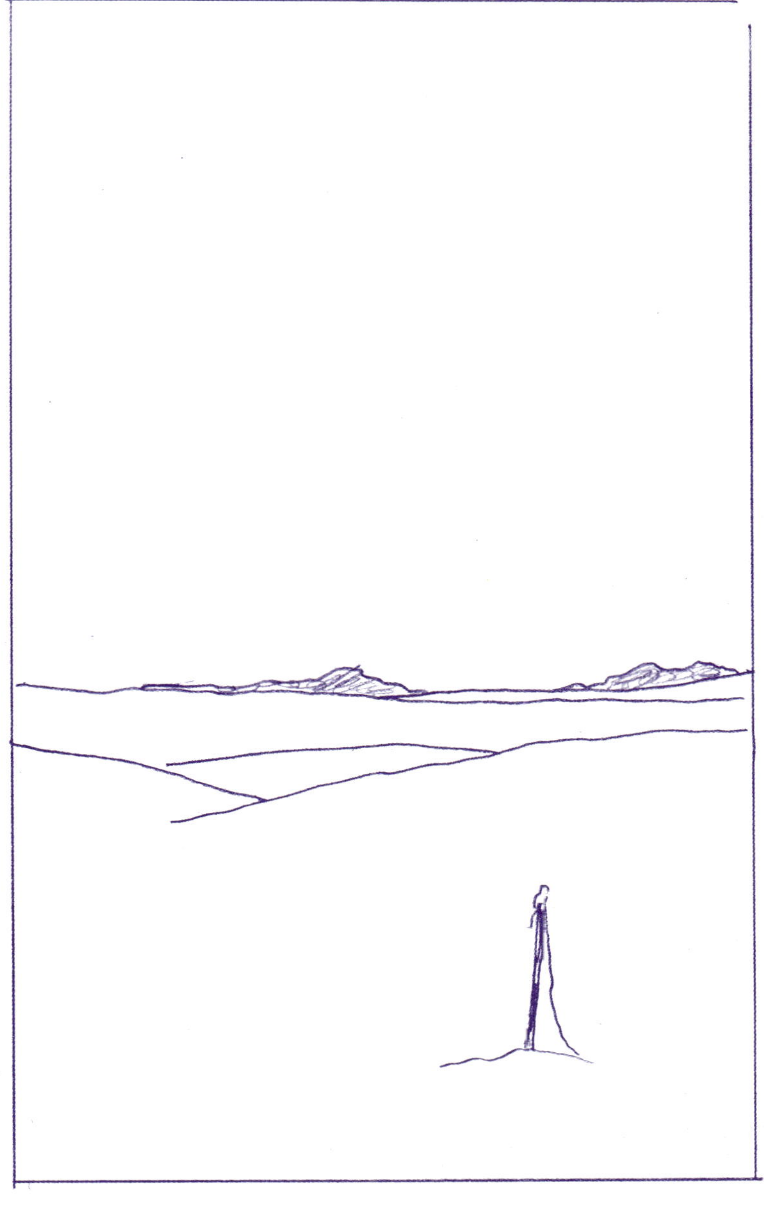

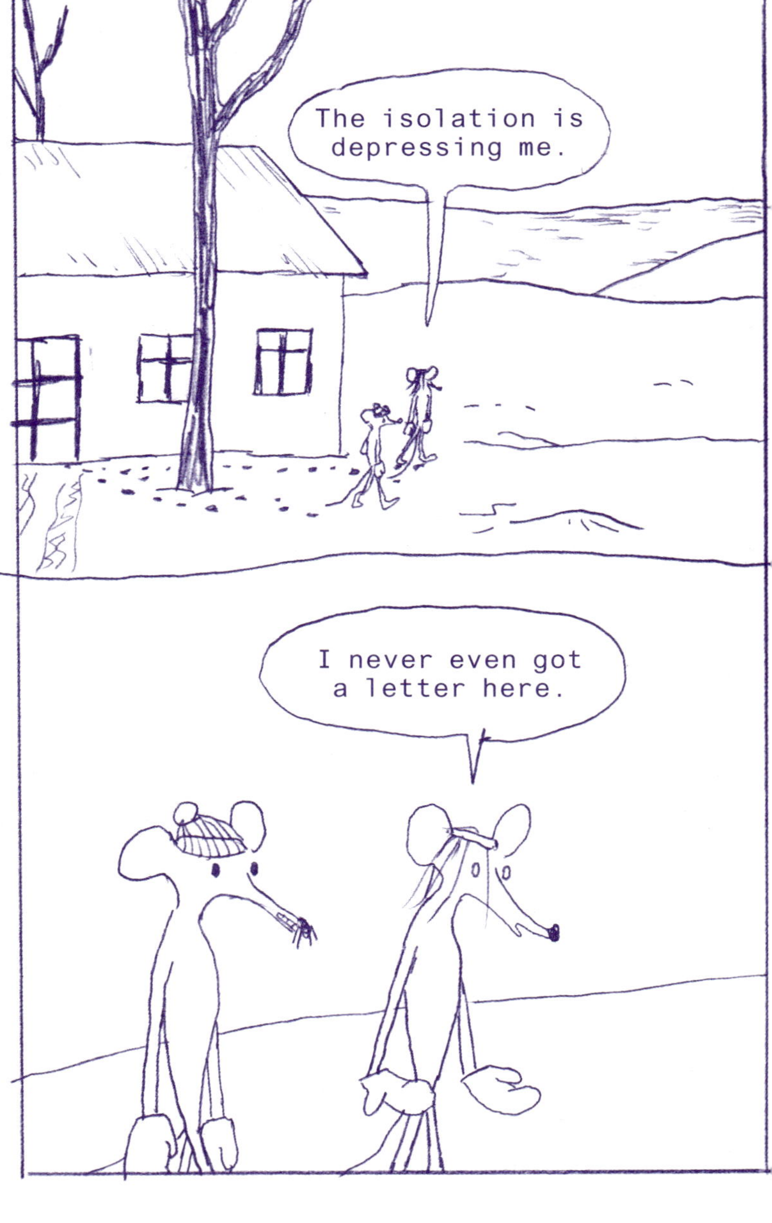

The isolation is depressing me.
I never even got a letter here.

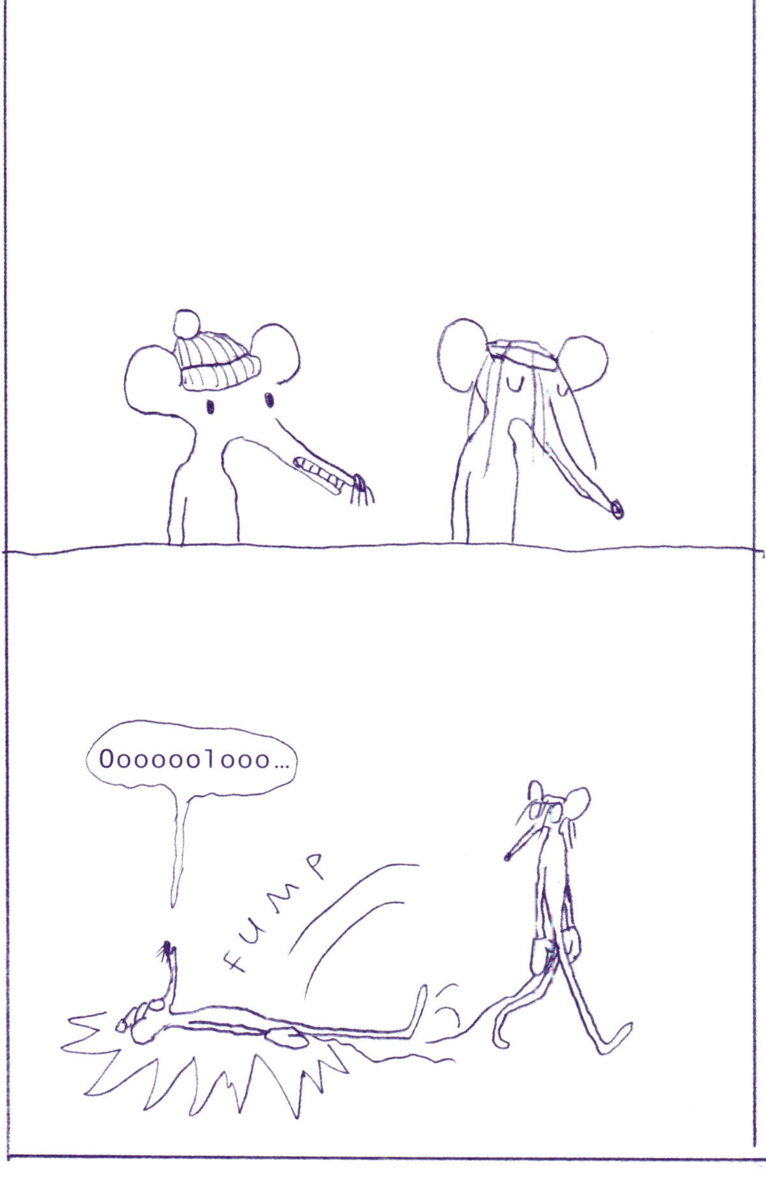
Oooooooloooo...
FUMP

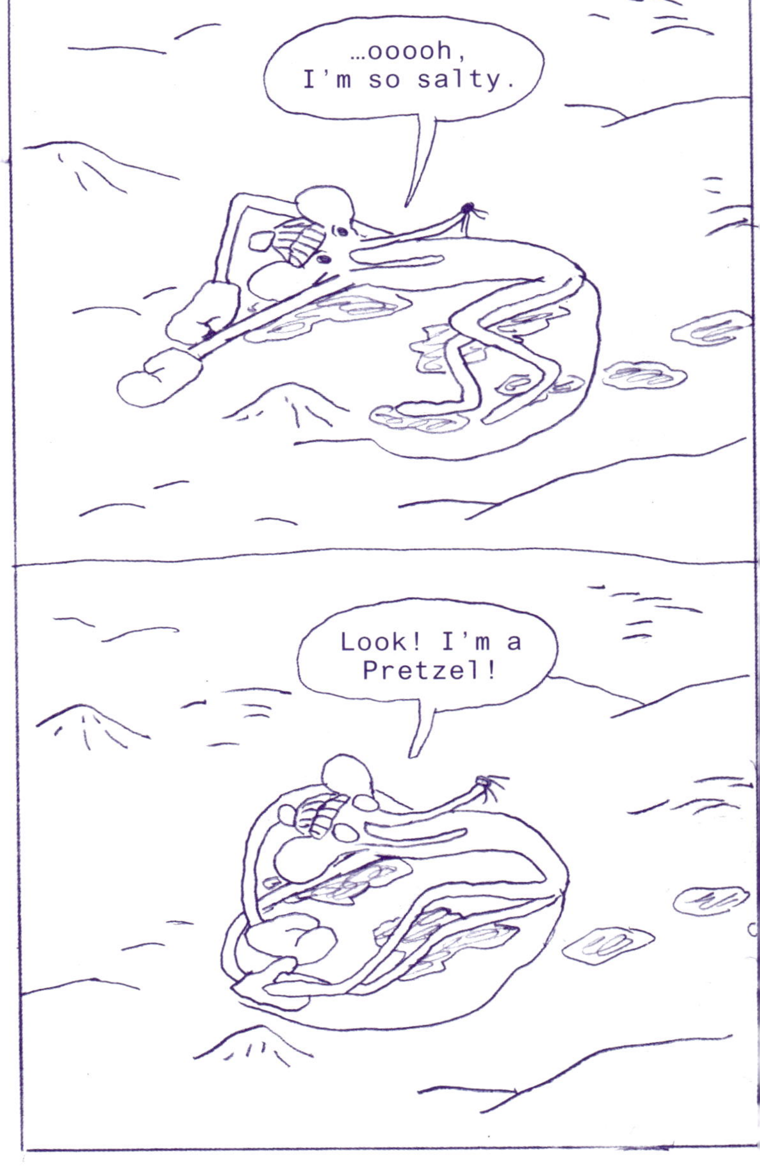
...ooooh,
I'm so salty.

Look! I'm a
Pretzel!

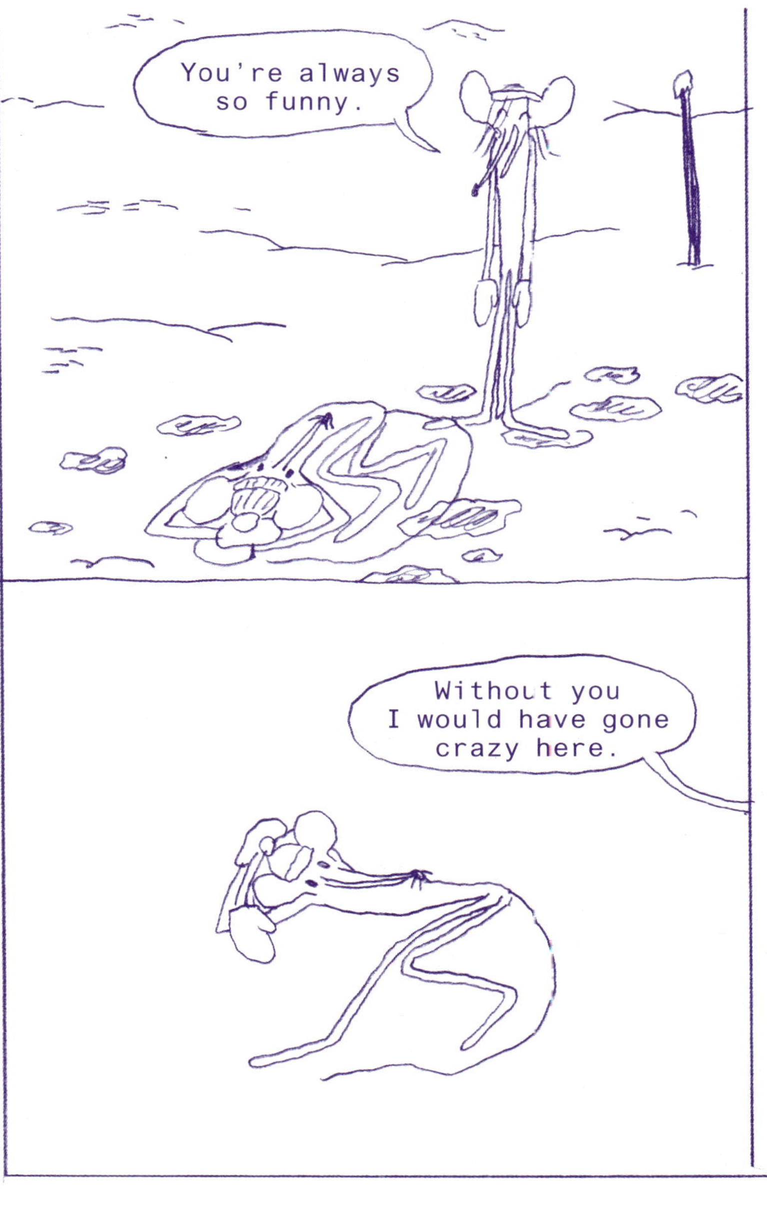

You're always so funny.
Without you I would have gone crazy here.

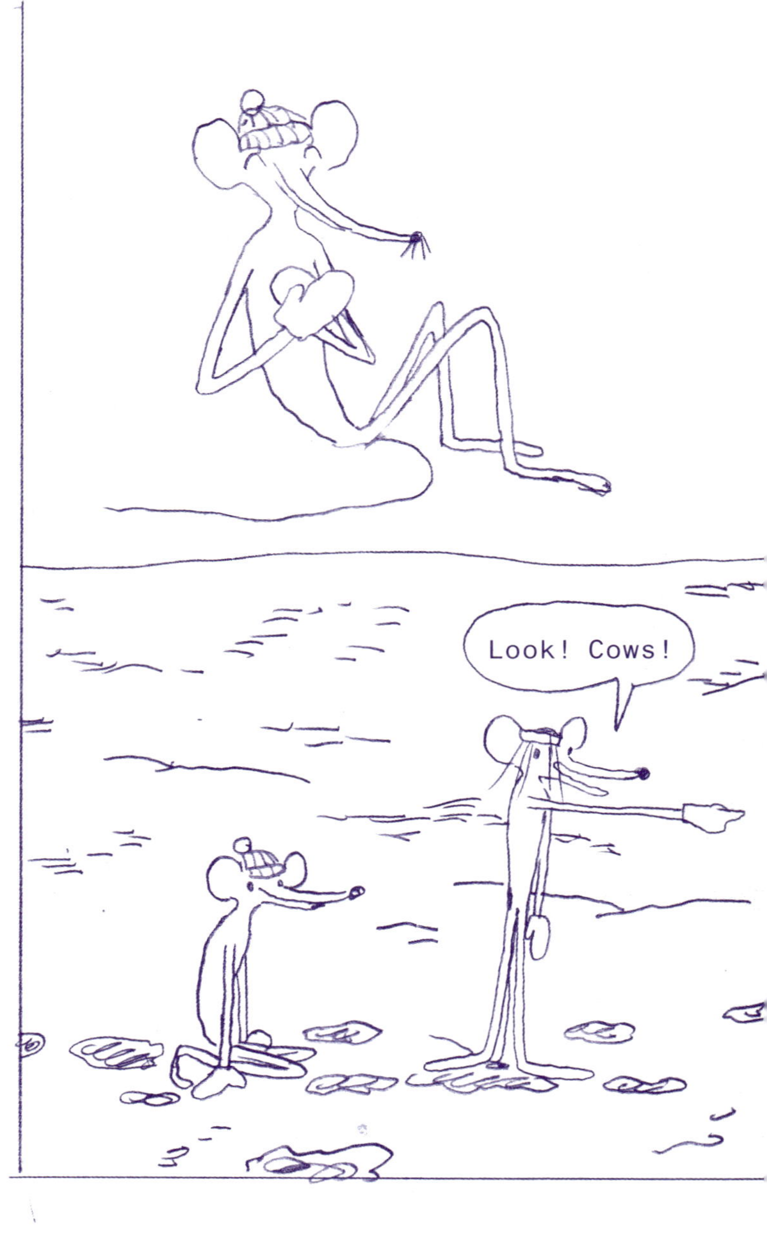

Look! Cows!

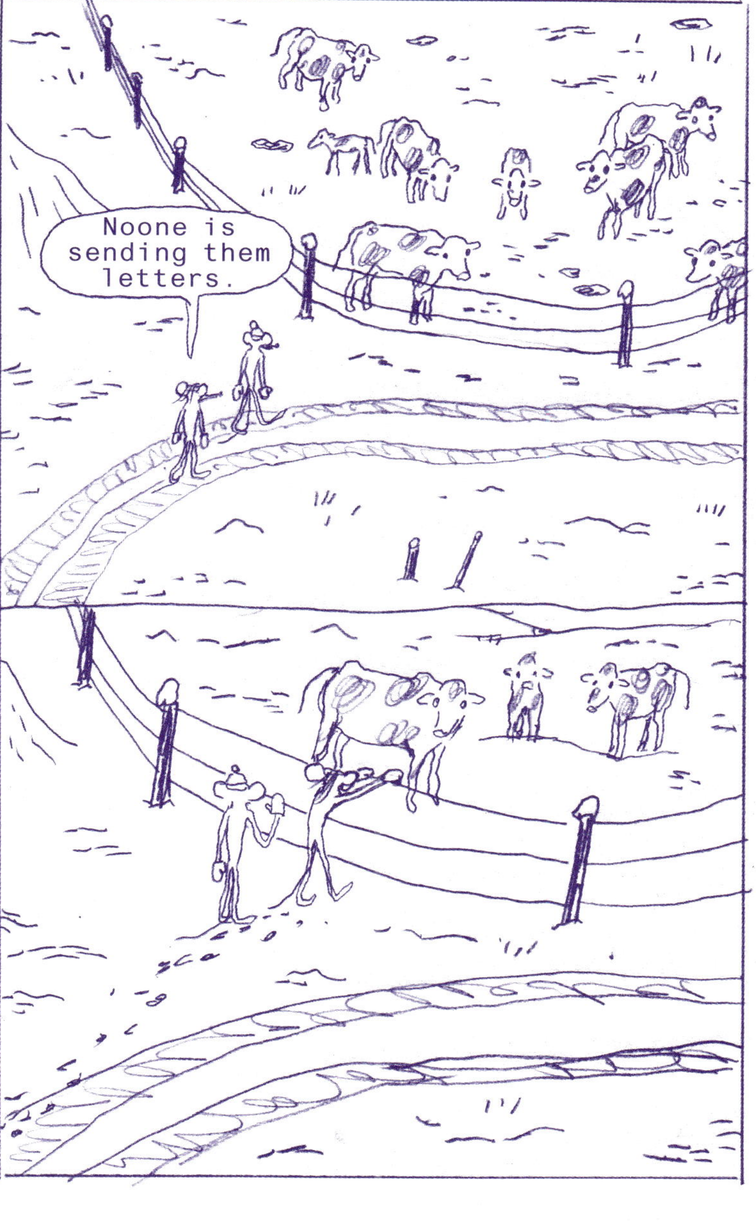

Noone is sending them letters.

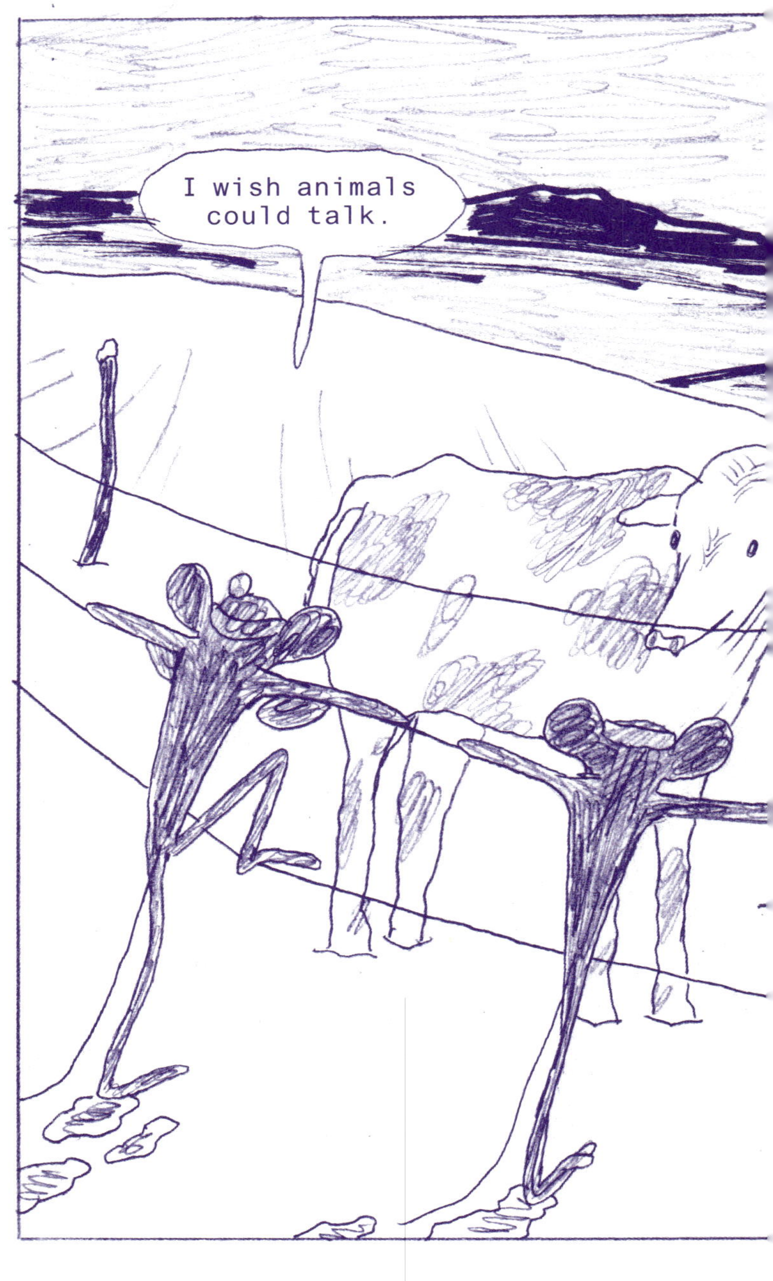
I wish animals
could talk.

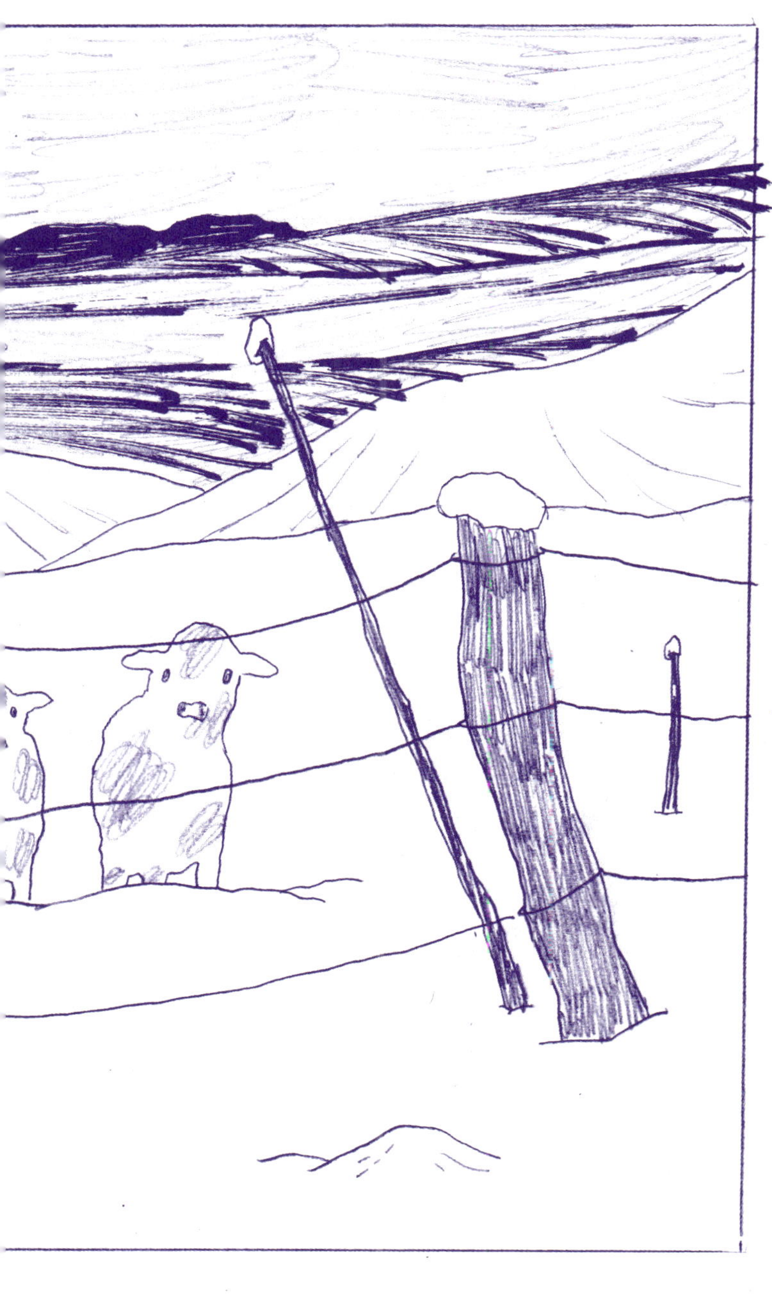

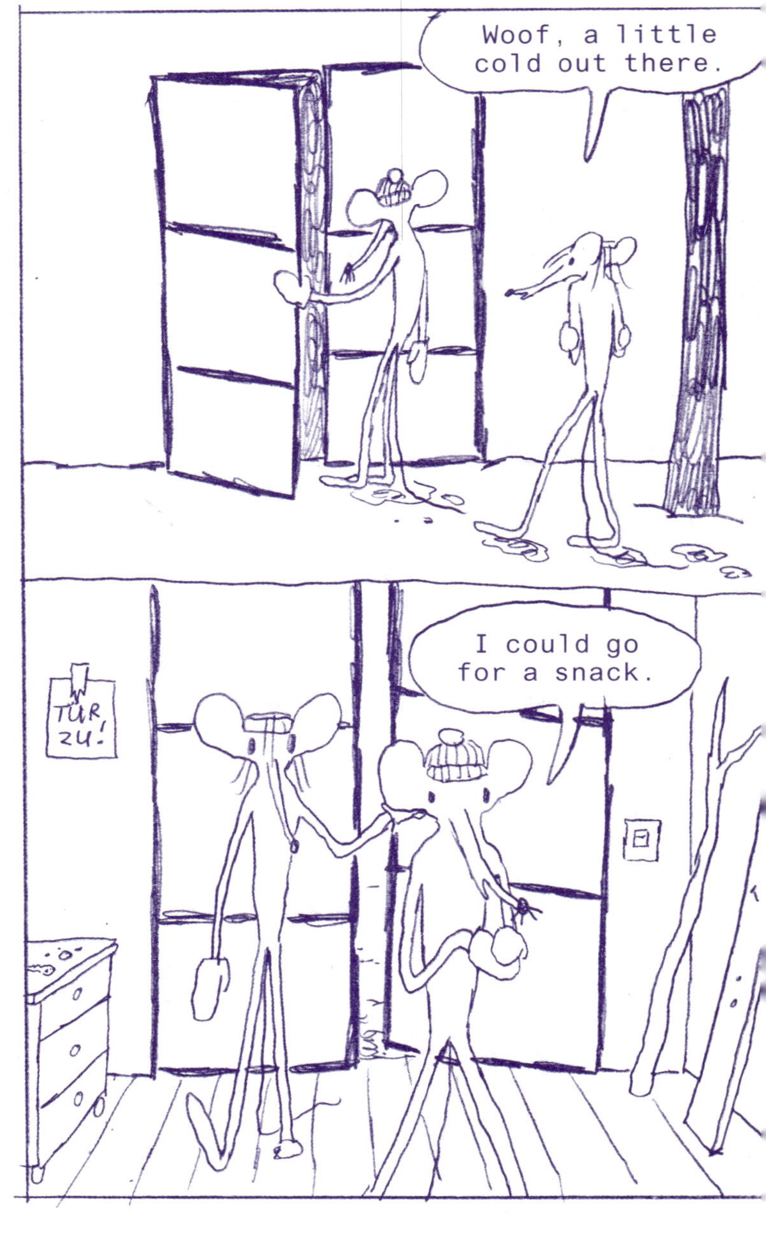

Woof, a little cold out there.
I could go for a snack.
TÜR ZU!

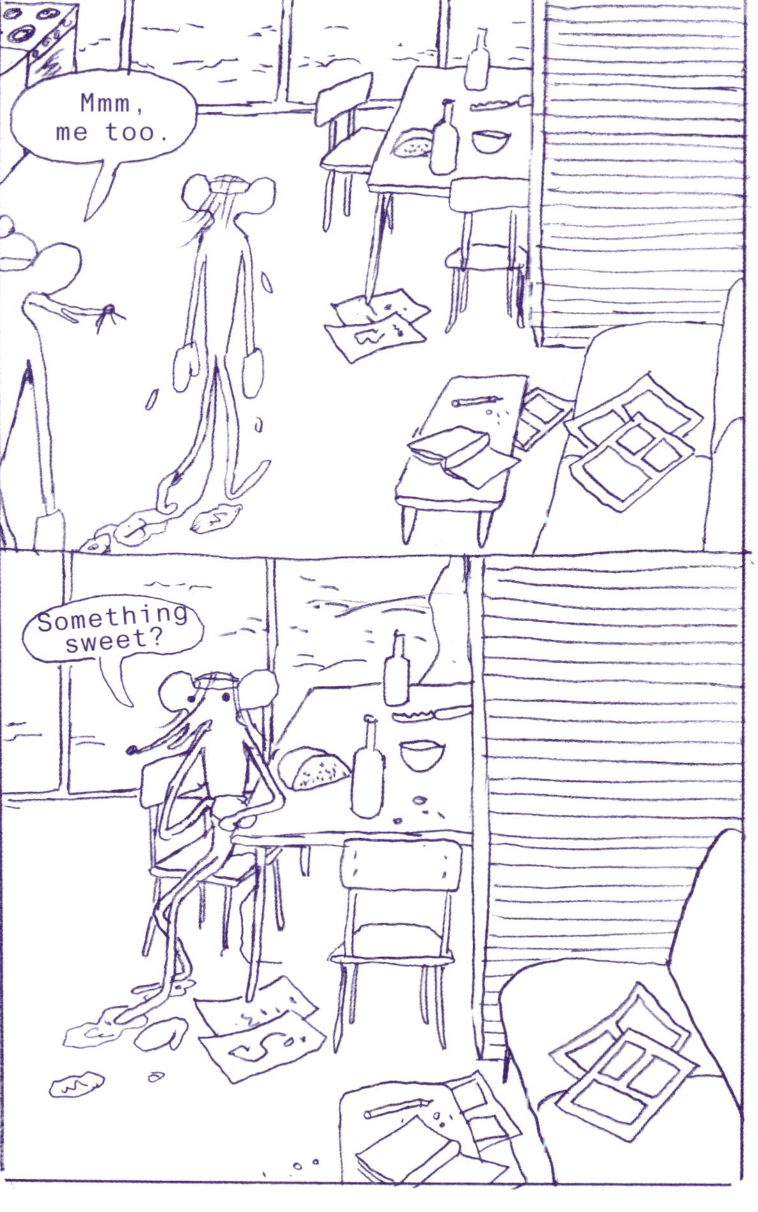

Mmm,
me too.

Something
sweet?

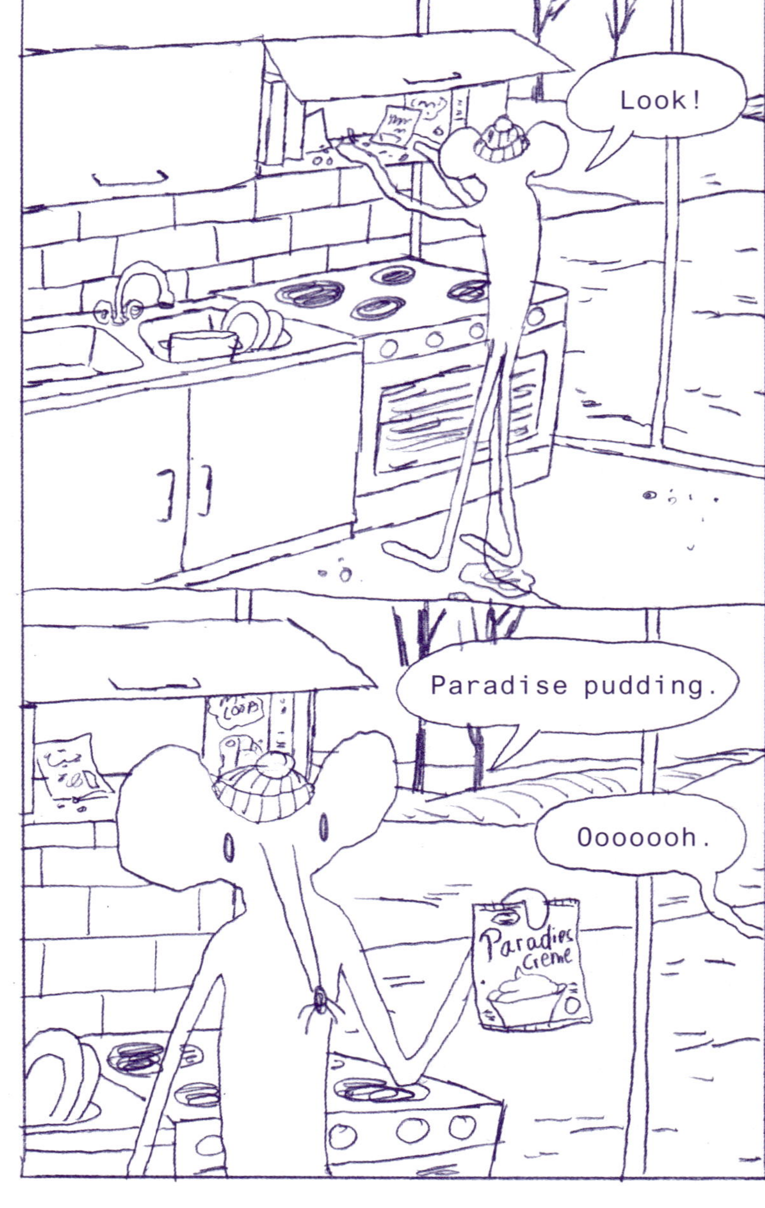

Look!
Paradise pudding.
Oooooooh.
Paradies Creme

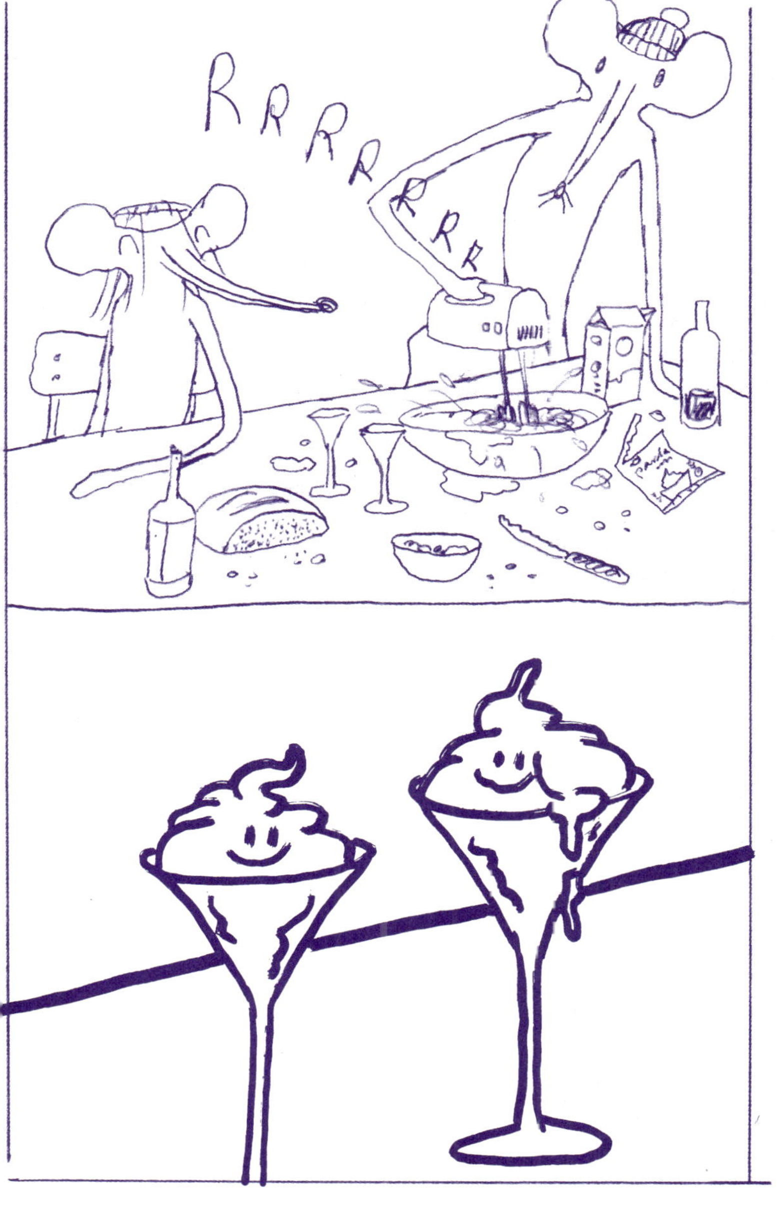

RRRRR
RRR

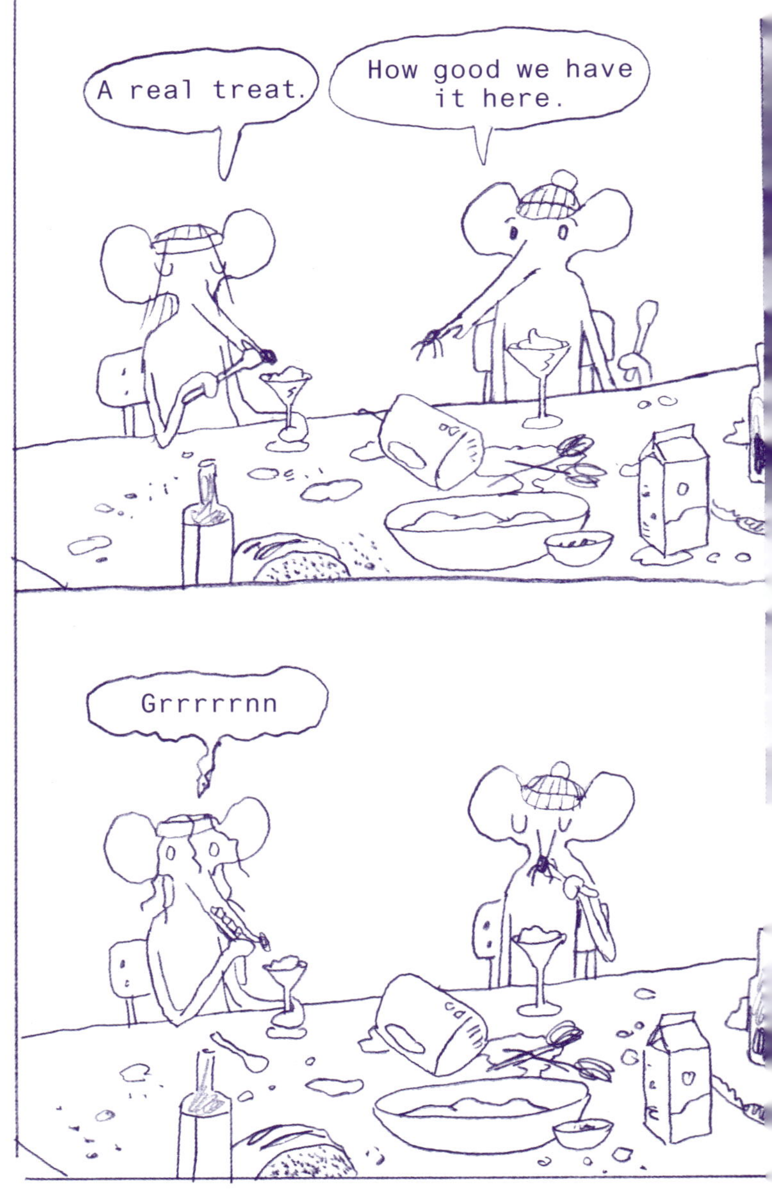

A real treat.
How good we have it here.
Grrrrrnn

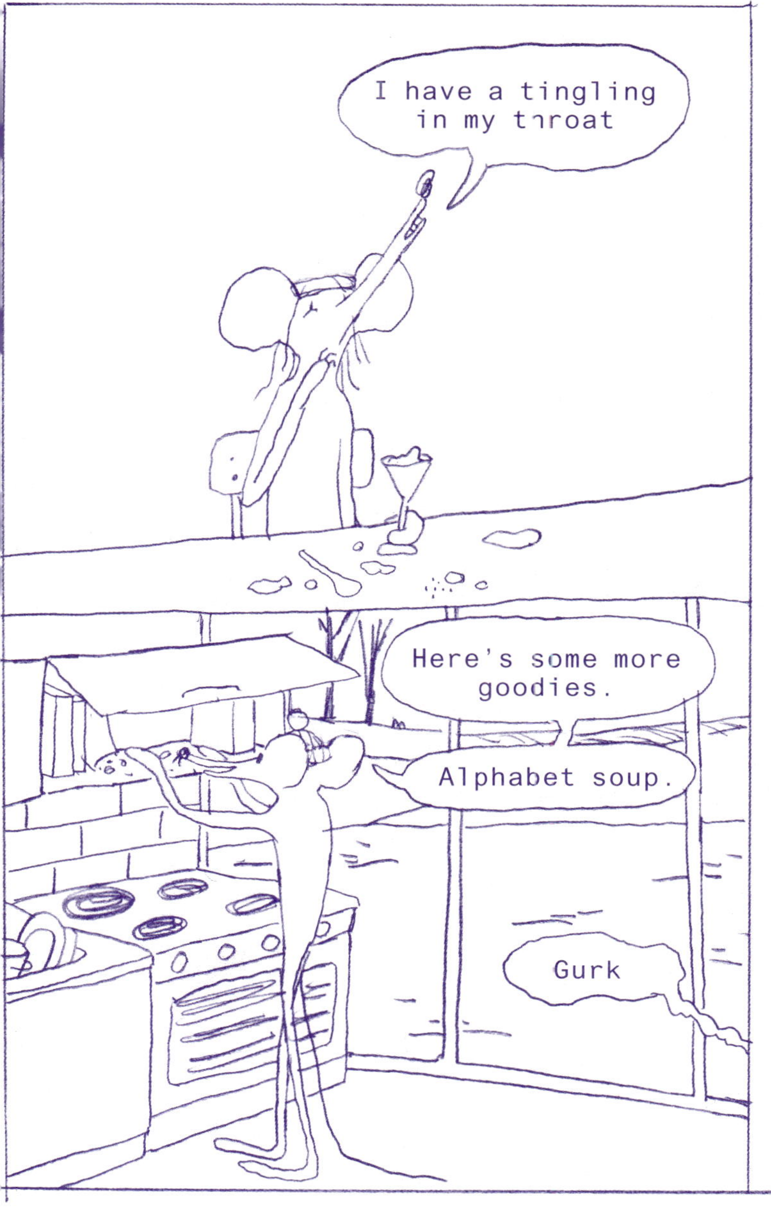
I have a tingling in my throat
Here's some more goodies.
Alphabet soup.
Gurk

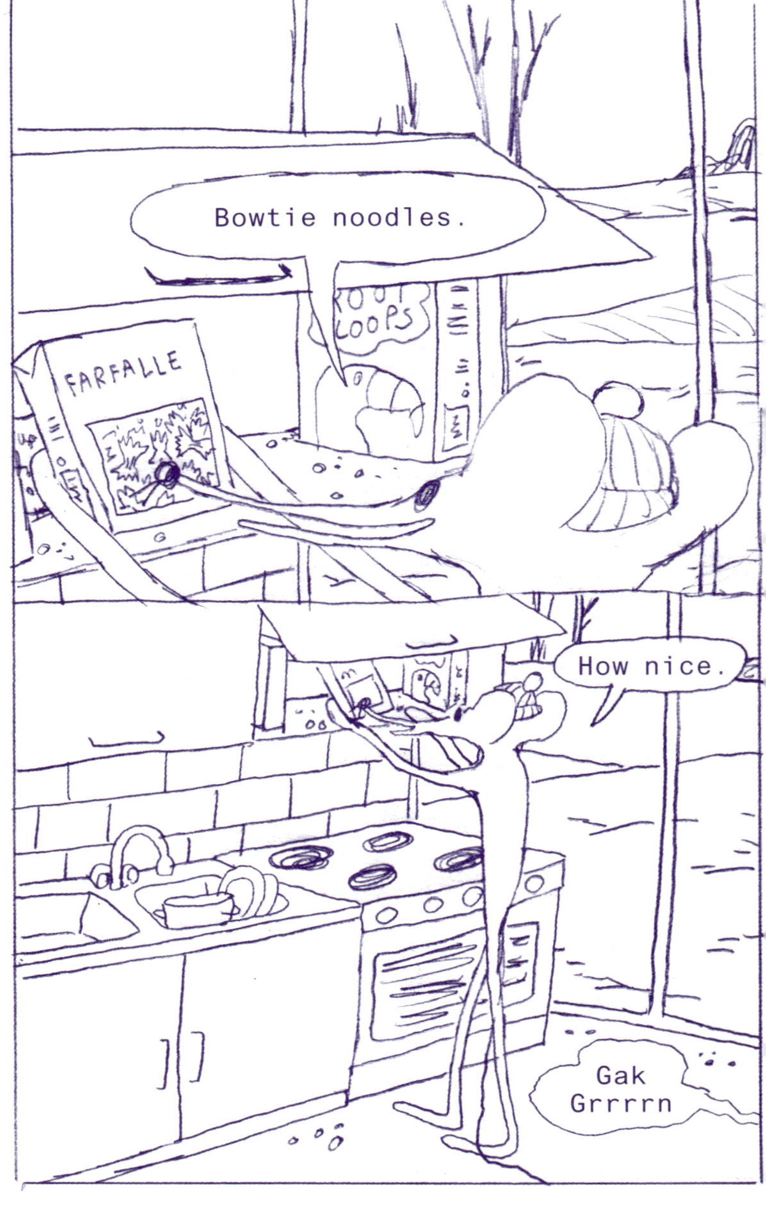

Bowtie noodles.
FARFALLE
OOPS
How nice.
Gak
Grrrrn

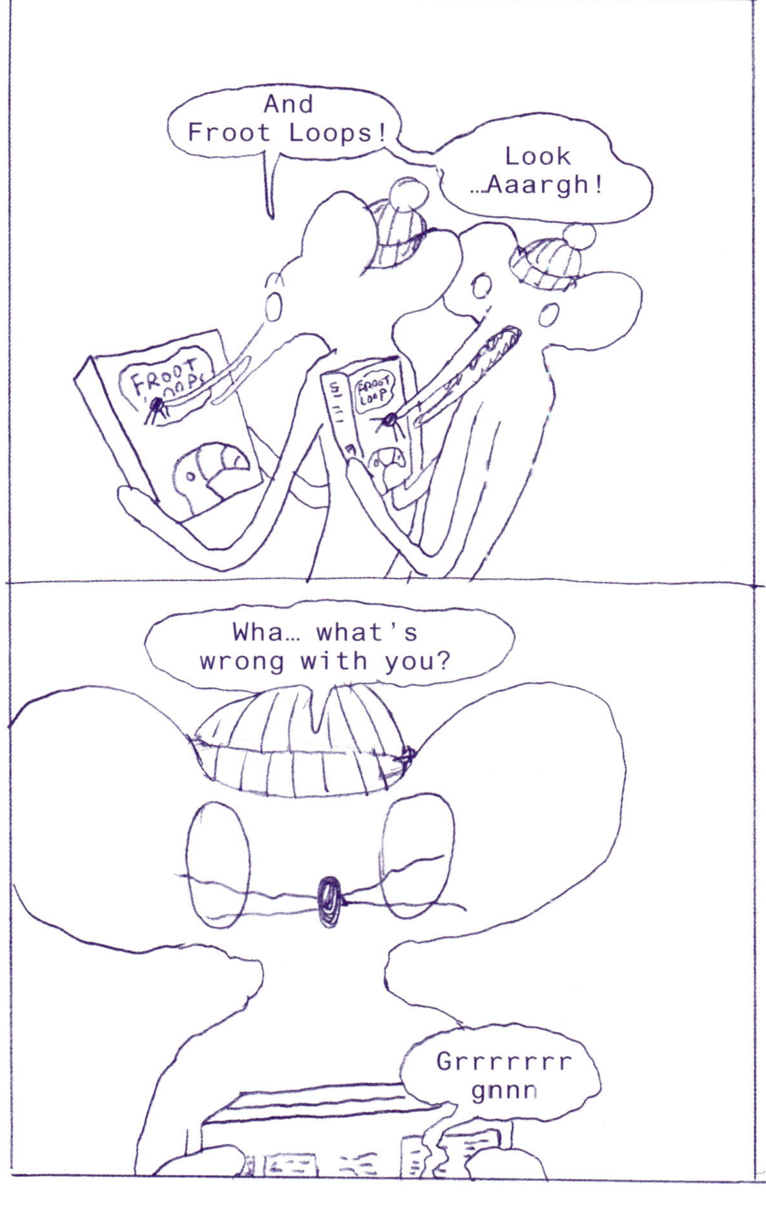

And
Froot Loops!
Look
...Aaargh!
Wha... what's
wrong with you?
Grrrrrrr
gnnn

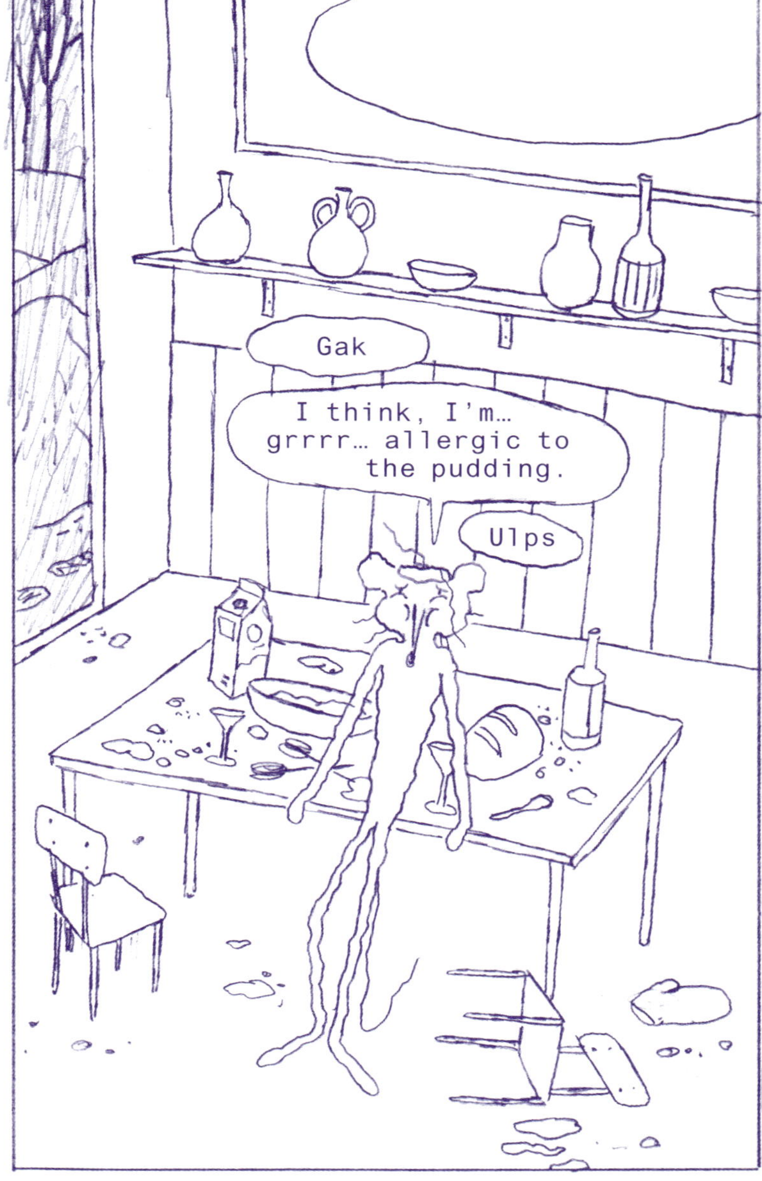

Gak
I think, I'm... grrrr... allergic to the pudding.
Ulps

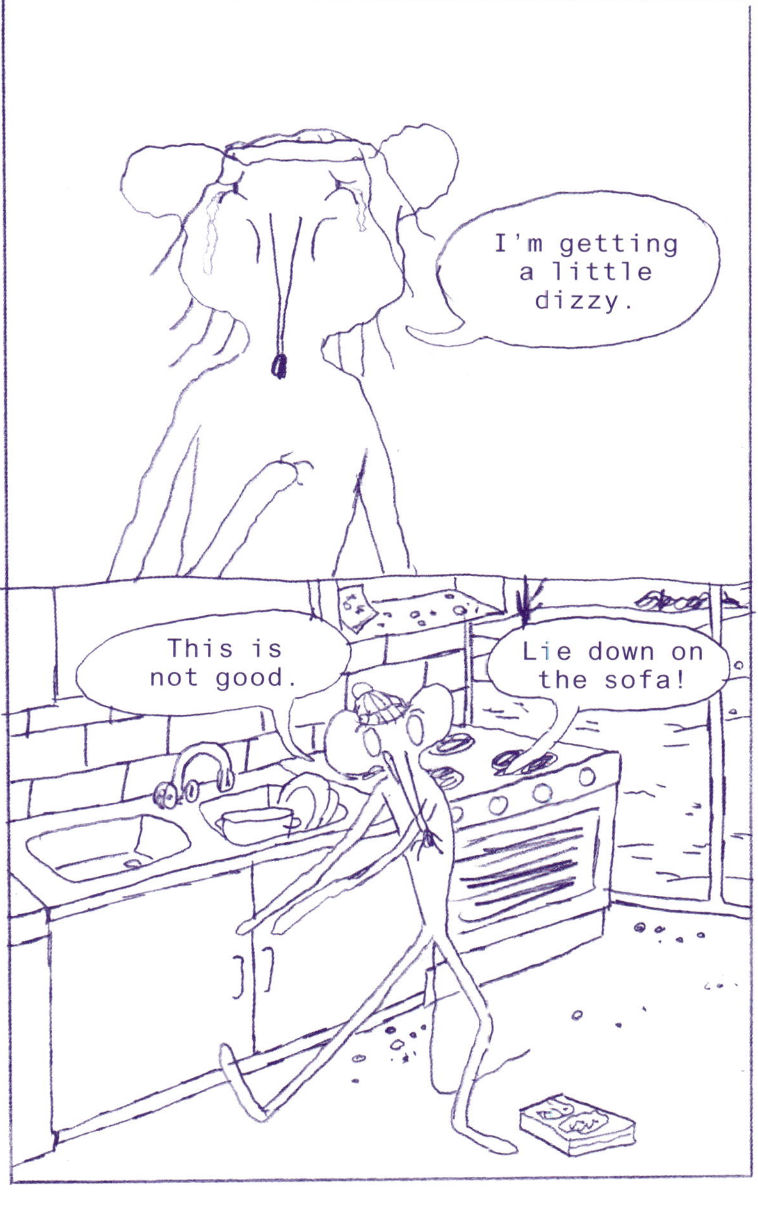

I'm getting a little dizzy.
This is not good.
Lie down on the sofa!

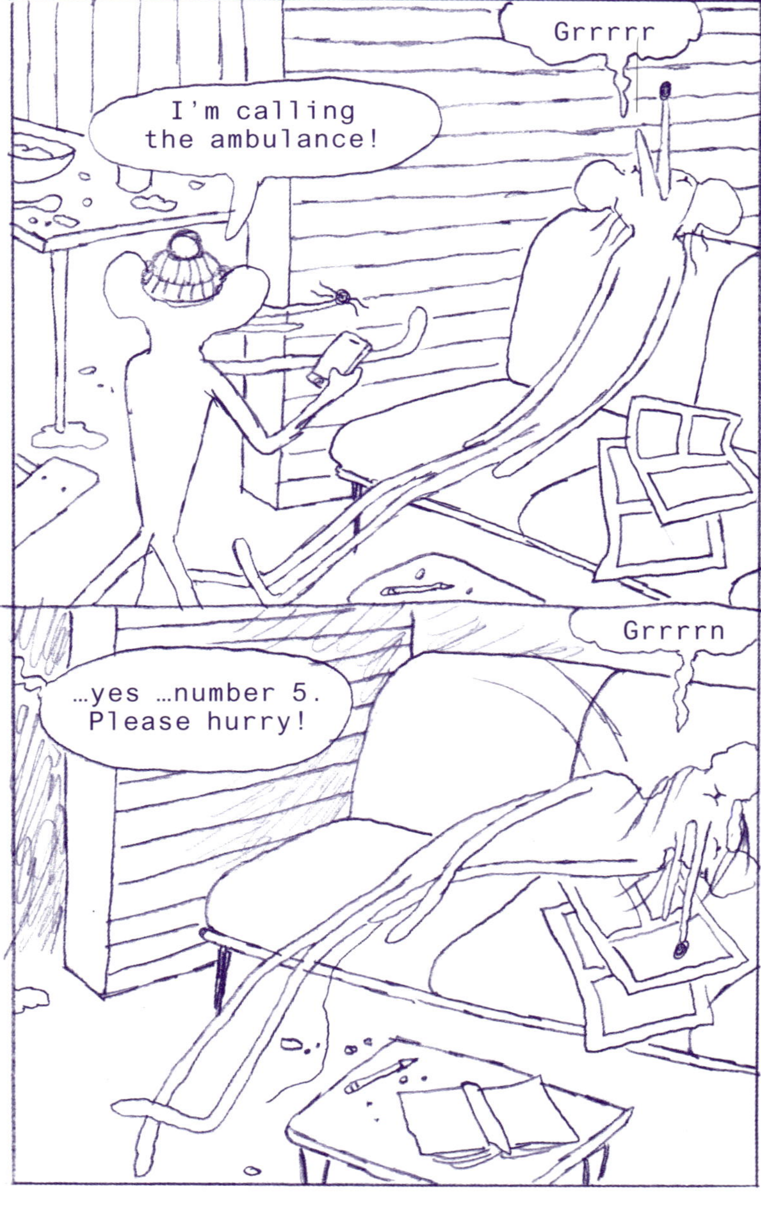

Grrrrr
I'm calling the ambulance!
Grrrrn
...yes ...number 5. Please hurry!

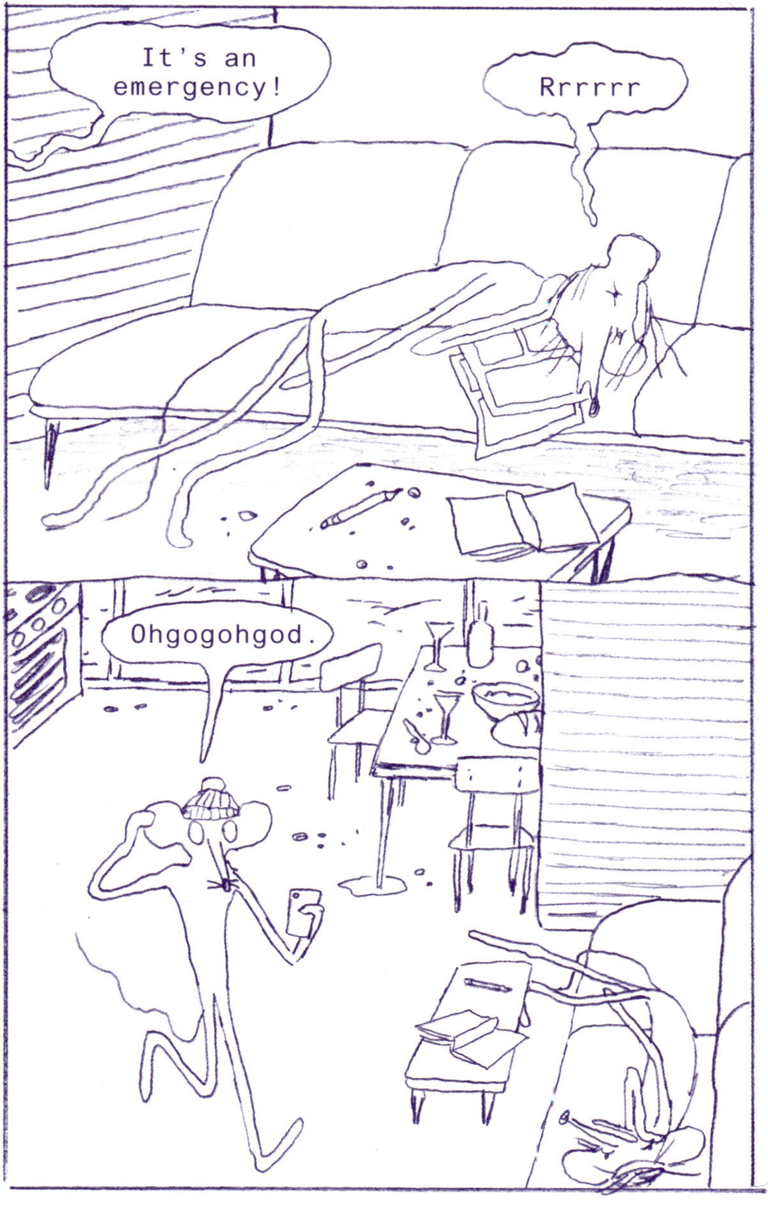

It's an
emergency!
Rrrrrr
Ohgogohgod.

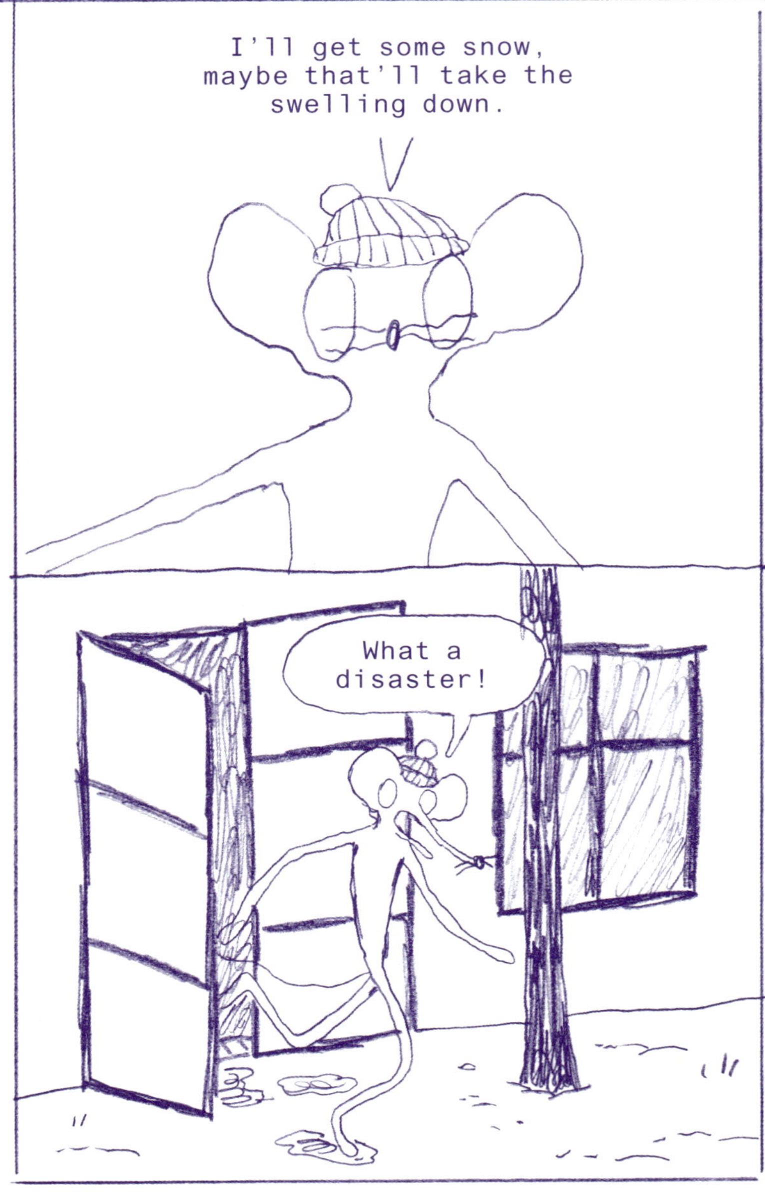

I'll get some snow, maybe that'll take the swelling down.
What a disaster!

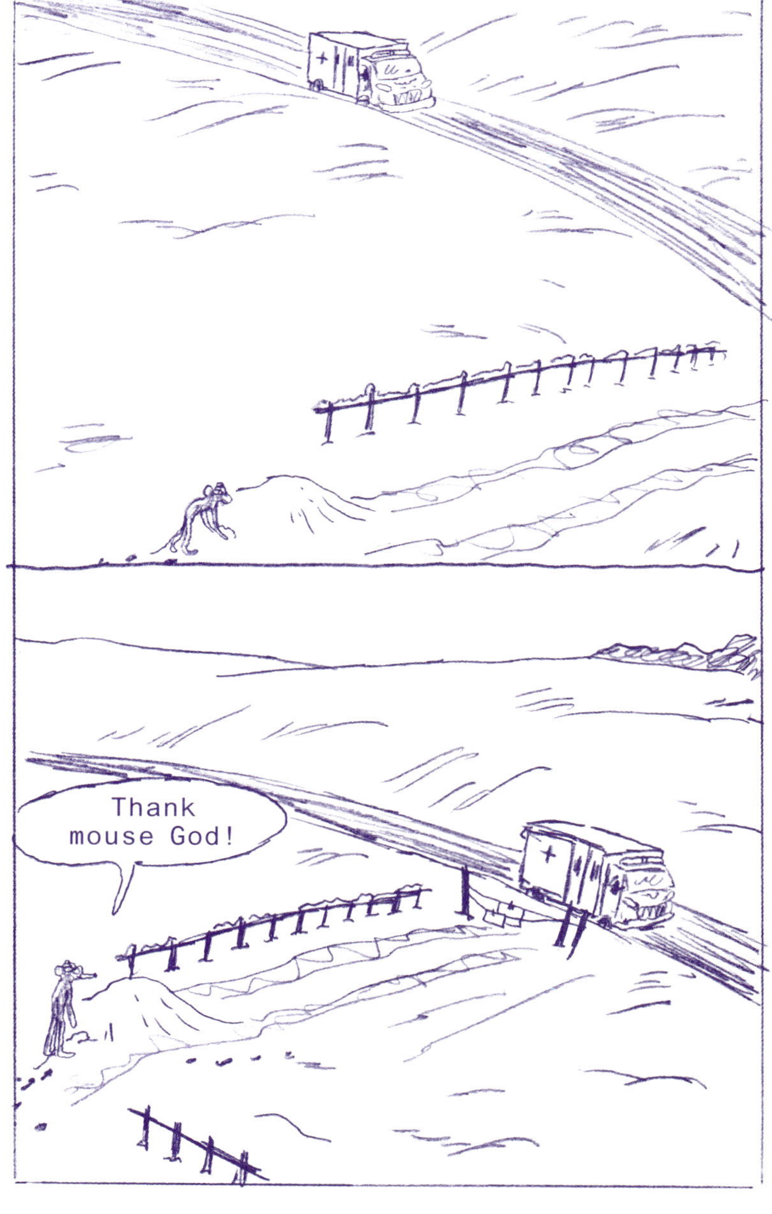
Thank
mouse God!

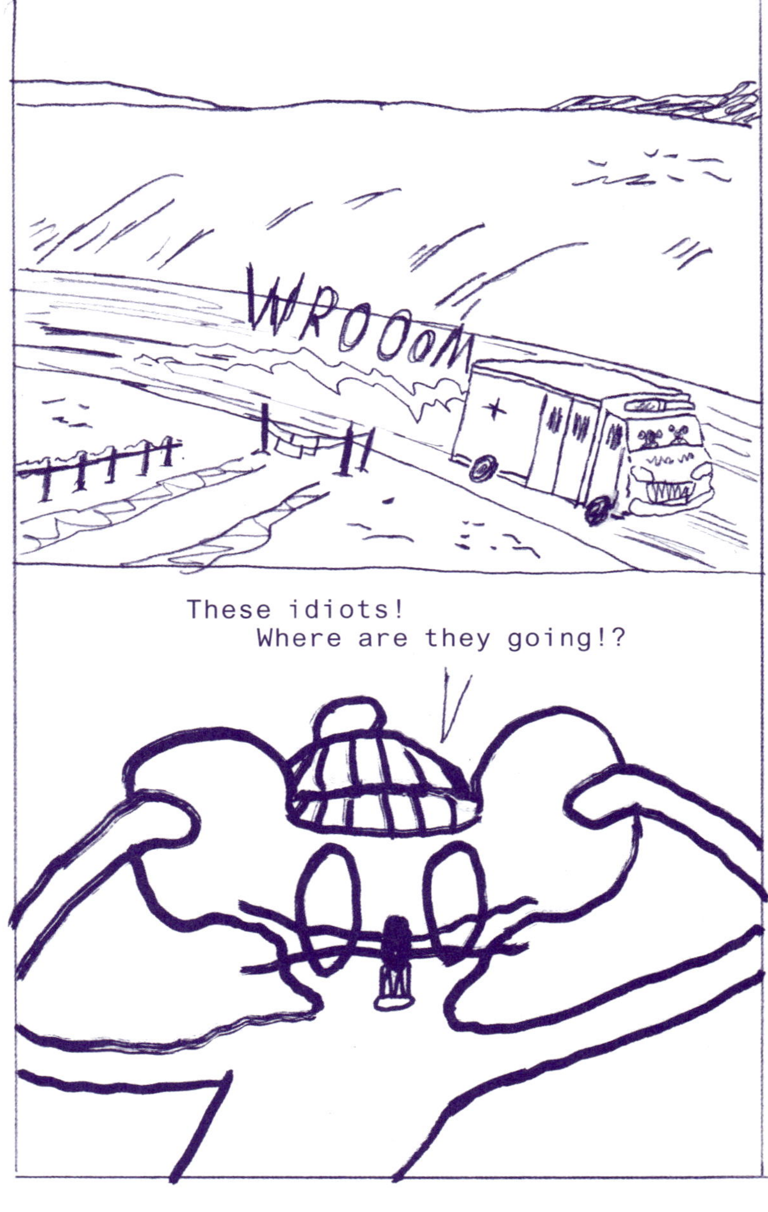

WROOOM
These idiots!
Where are they going!?

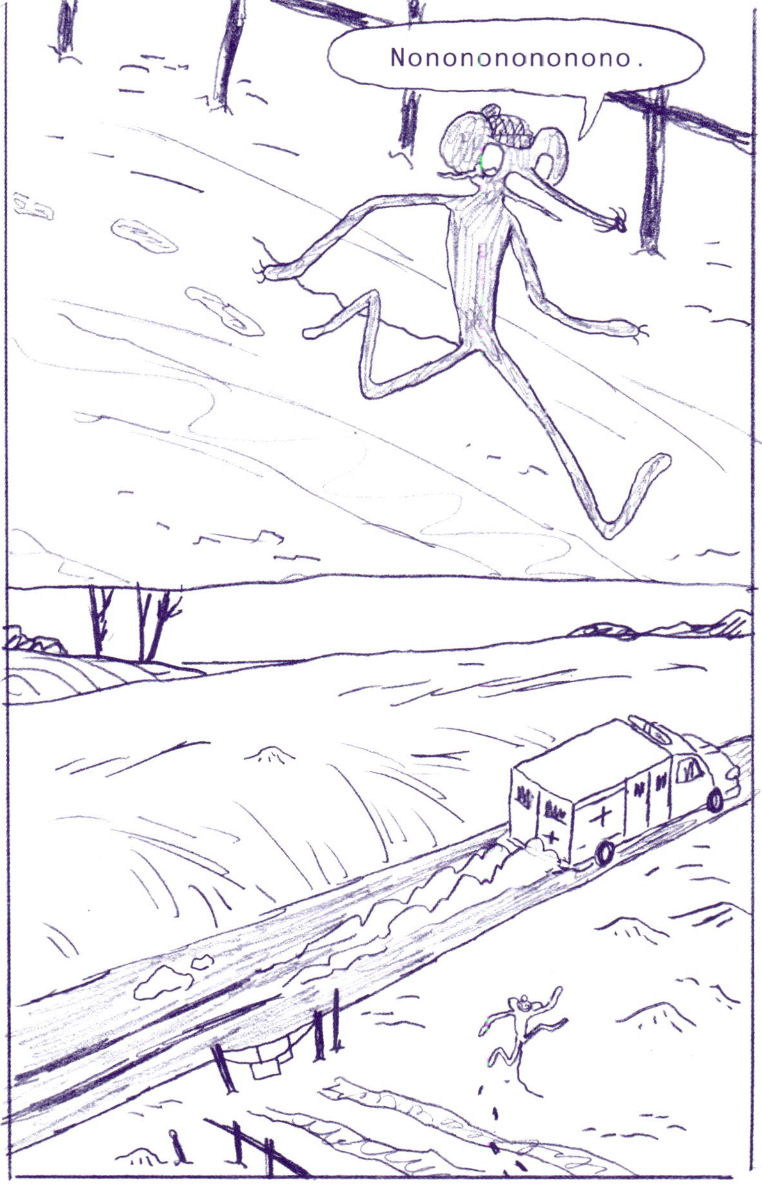

Nononononononono.

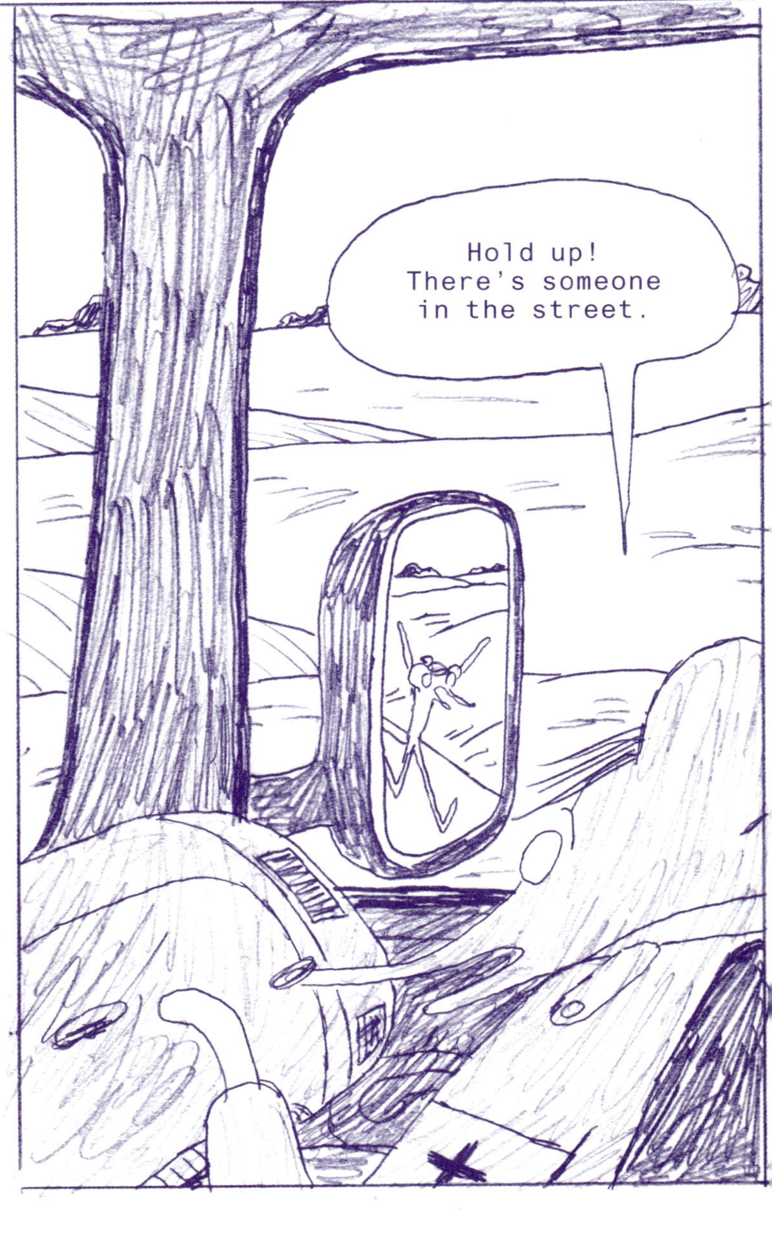

Hold up!
There's someone
in the street.

Mouse in Residence

I intended to write and draw this book in an artist residency in Columbus, Ohio in the fall of 2020. This became impossible because of Corona. The book was subsequently created in Leipzig, Germany during the second Lockdown. The atmosphere of mental collapse created a good foundation for this story.

Fahrenbuhl is nearly a fictional place. There is the Fahrenbühl Hunting Lodge in Kirchlamitz, Germany near to the Erika Fuchs House, the Museum of Comics and Literary Language. I can highly recommend spending a weekend there. Don't forget your hunting rifle.

My Fahrenbuhl is located in the fictional Cole Mountain region. Bernd Schirmer wrote the novel Cole Mountain (Cahlenberg, Connewitzer Verlagsbuchhandlung, 1994) about a mysterious remote area, that spoke to me as a setting for this book.

Many thanks to Mathias Zeiske, Jan Wenzel, James Turek, Aeni Kaiser and the Cultural Foundation of the State of Saxony.

Anna   January 2021

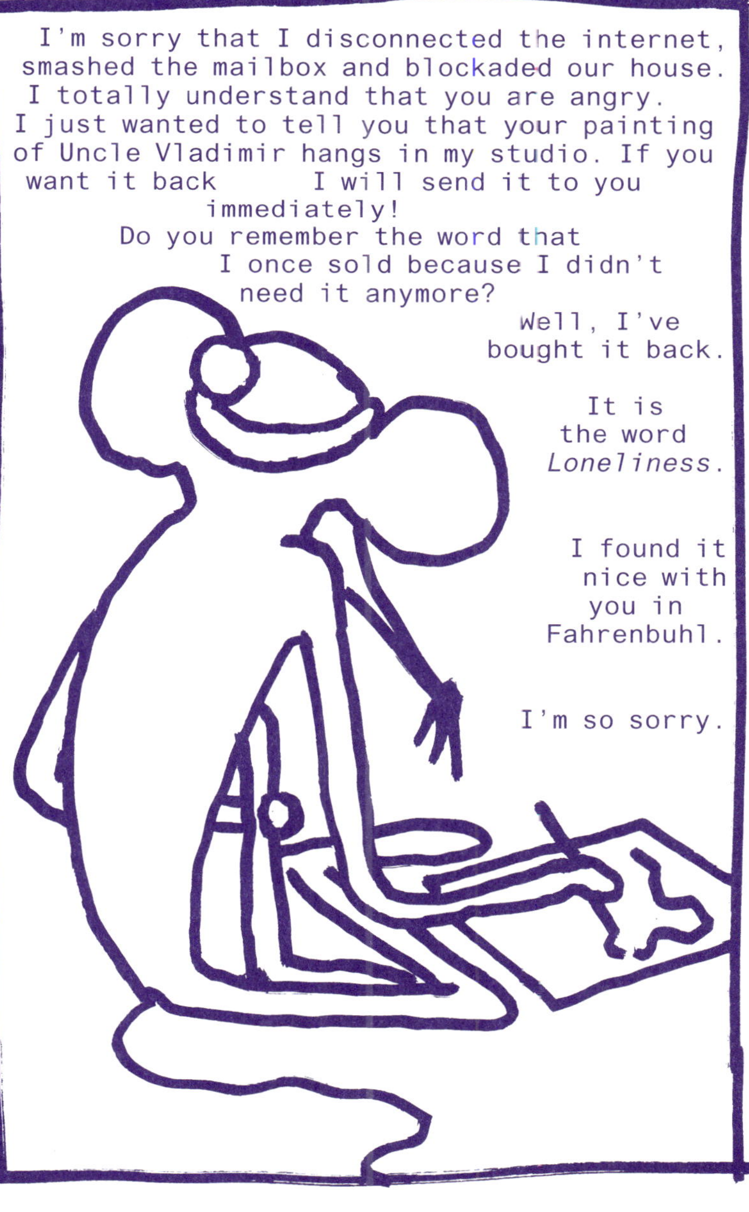

I'm sorry that I disconnected the internet, smashed the mailbox and blockaded our house. I totally understand that you are angry. I just wanted to tell you that your painting of Uncle Vladimir hangs in my studio. If you want it back   I will send it to you immediately!
Do you remember the word that I once sold because I didn't need it anymore?
Well, I've bought it back.
It is the word Loneliness.
I found it nice with you in Fahrenbuhl.
I'm so sorry.

Anna Haifisch
Mouse in Residence

Translation: James Turek
Typeface: DeVille, Grilli Type/Arial Monospaced
Typography: Hannes Drißner

© 2021 Anna Haifisch and Spector Books

Published by Spector Books, Leipzig
www.spectorbooks.com

Distribution:
GERMANY, AUSTRIA: GVA Gemeinsame Verlagsauslieferung
    Göttingen GmbH & Co. KG, www.gva-verlage.de
SWITZERLAND: AVA Verlagsauslieferung AG, www.ava.ch
FRANCE, BELGIUM: Interart Paris, www.interart.fr
UK: Central Books Ltd, www.centralbooks.com
USA, CANADA, CENTRAL AND SOUTH AMERICA, AFRICA:
    ARTBOOK | D.A.P. www.artbook.com
JAPAN: twelvebooks, www.twelve-books.com
SOUTH KOREA: The Book Society, www.thebooksociety.org
AUSTRALIA, NEW ZEALAND: Perimeter Distribution,
    www.perimeterdistribution.com

Printed in Germany
ISBN: 978-3-95905-503-1

Second Edition, 2025

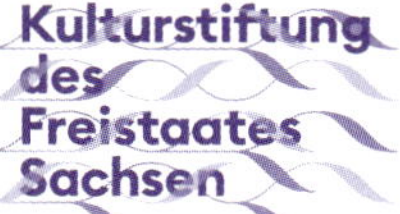 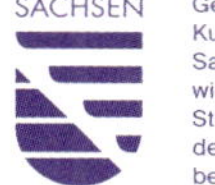 Gefördert durch die Kulturstiftung des Freistaates Sachsen. Diese Maßnahme wird mitfinanziert durch Steuermittel auf der Grundlage des vom Sächsischen Landtag beschlossenen Haushaltes.

Anna Haifisch (*1986) is an artist
from Leipzig, Germany. She drew
the comic series "The Artist" for
The Museum of Modern Art New
York, Le Monde and Vice.

Her comic books are translated in
several languages.

www.hai-life.com